POEMS

OF

ELIZABETH BARRETT BROWNING.

THE

POEMS

OF

ELIZABETH BARRETT BROWNING.

A NEW EDITION,

CAREFULLY CORRECTED BY THE LAST LONDON EDITION.

WITH AN INTRODUCTORY ESSAY.

VOL. II.

NEW YORK:
C. S. FRANCIS & CO., 252 BROADWAY.
BOSTON: CROSBY & NICHOLS.
M.DCCC.LIII.

CONTENTS OF VOL. II.

A DRAMA OF EXILE.

A DRAMA OF EXILE.

PERSONS OF THE DRAMA.

ADAM.	LUCIFER.	Earth Spirits and Phantasms.
EVE.	Angels.	The Morning Star.
GABRIEL.	Eden Spirits.	CHRIST, in a Vision.

SCENE—*The outer side of the gate of Eden shut fast with clouds, from the depth of which revolves the sword of fire, self-moved. A watch of innumerable* ANGELS, *rank above rank, slopes up from around it to the zenith; and the glare, cast from their brightness and from the sword, extends many miles into the wilderness.* ADAM *and* EVE *are seen in the distance, flying along the glare. The* ANGEL GABRIEL *and* LUCIFER *are beside the gate.*

Lucifer. Hail Gabriel, the keeper of the gate!
Now that the fruit is plucked, prince Gabriel,
I hold that Eden is impregnable
Under thy keeping.
Gabriel. Angel of the sin,
Such as thou standest,—pale in the drear light
Which rounds the rebel's work with Maker's wrath,—
Thou shalt be an Idea to all souls;—
A monumental melancholy gloom
Seen down all ages; whence to mark despair,
And measure out the distances from good!
Go from us straightway.

Lucifer. Wherefore?

Gabriel. Lucifer,
Thy last step in this place, trod sorrow up.
Recoil before that sorrow, if not this sword.

Lucifer. Angels are in the world—wherefore not I?
Exiles are in the world—wherefore not I?
The cursed are in the world—wherefore not I?

Gabriel. Depart.

Lucifer. And where's the logic of "depart?"
Our lady Eve had half been satisfied
To obey her Maker, if I had not learnt
To fix my postulate better. Dost thou dream
Of guarding some monopoly in heaven
Instead of earth? Why I can dream with thee
To the length of thy wings.

Gabriel. I do not dream.
This is not Heaven, even in a dream; nor earth,
As earth was once,—first breathed among the stars,—
Articulate glory from the mouth divine,—
To which the myriad spheres thrilled audibly,
Touched like a lute-string,—and the sons of God
Said AMEN, singing it. I know that this
Is earth, not new created, but new cursed—
This, Eden's gate, not opened, but built up
With a final cloud of sunset. Do I dream?
Alas, not so! this is the Eden lost
By Lucifer the serpent! this the sword
(This sword, alive with justice and with fire!)
That smote upon the forehead, Lucifer
The angel! Wherefore, angel, go . . . depart—
Enough is sinned and suffered.

Lucifer. By no means.
Here's a brave earth to sin and suffer on!
It holds fast still—it cracks not under curse;
It holds, like mine immortal. Presently
We 'll sow it thick enough with graves as green
Or greener, certes, than its knowledge-tree—
We 'll have the cypress for the tree of life,
More eminent for shadow—for the rest
We 'll build it dark with towns and pyramids,
And temples, if it please you:—we 'll have feasts
And funerals also, merrymakes and wars,
Till blood and wine shall mix and run along
Right o'er the edges. And, good Gabriel,
(Ye like that word in Heaven!) *I* too have strength—
Strength to behold Him, and not worship Him;
Strength to fall from Him, and not cry on Him;
Strength to be in the universe, and yet
Neither God nor his servant. The red sign
Burnt on my forehead, which you taunt me with,
Is God's sign that it bows not unto God;
The potter's mark upon his work, to show
It rings well to the striker. I and the earth
Can bear more curse.
Gabriel. O miserable earth!
O ruined angel!
Lucifer. Well! and if it be,
I CHOSE this ruin: I elected it
Of my will, not of service. What I do,
I do volitient, not obedient,
And overtop thy crown with my despair.
My sorrow crowns me. Get thee back to Heaven;

And leave me to the earth, which is mine own
In virtue of her misery, as I hers,
In virtue of my ruin! turn from both,
That bright, impassive, passive angelhood;
And spare to read us backward any more
Of your spent hallelujahs.

Gabriel. Spirit of scorn!
I might say, of unreason! I might say,
That who despairs, acts; that who acts, connives
With God's relations set in time and space;
That who elects, assumes a something good
Which God made possible; that who lives, obeys
The law of a Life-maker . . .

Lucifer. Let it pass!
No more, thou Gabriel! What if I stand up
And strike my brow against the crystaline
Roofing the creatures,—shall I say for that,
My stature is too high for me to stand,—
Henceforward I must sit? Sit *thou.*

Gabriel. I kneel.

Lucifer. A heavenly answer. Get thee to thy
Heaven,
And leave my earth to me.

Gabriel. Through Heaven and earth
God's will moves freely; and I follow it,
As color follows light. He overflows
The firmamental walls with Deity,
Therefore with love: His lightnings go abroad,
His pity may do so; His angels must,
Whene'er He gives them charges.

Lucifer. Verily,

I and my demons—who are spirits of scorn—
Might hold this charge of standing with a sword
'Twixt man and his inheritance, as well
As the benignest angel of you all.

Gabriel. Thou speakest in the shadow of thy change.
If thou hadst gazed upon the face of God
This morning for a moment, thou hadst known
That only pity fitly can chastise,
While hate avenges.

Lucifer As it is, I know
Something of pity. When I reeled in Heaven,
And my sword grew too heavy for my wrist,
Stabbing through matter, which it could not pierce
So much as the first shell of,—toward the throne;
When I fell back, down,—staring up as I fell,—
The lightnings holding open my scathed lids,
And that thought of the infinite of God
Drawn from the finite, speeding my descent;
When countless angel-faces, still and stern,
Pressed out upon me from the level heavens,
Adown the abysmal spaces; and I fell,
Trampled down by your stillness, and struck blind
By the sight in your eyes;—'twas then I knew
How ye could pity, my kind angelhood!

Gabriel. Yet, thou discrowned one, by the truth in me
Which God keeps in me, I would give away
All,—save that truth, and His love over it,—
To lead thee home again into the light,

And hear thy voice chant with the morning stars;
When their rays tremble round them with much song,
Sung in more gladness!

Lucifer. Sing, my morning star!
Last beautiful—last heavenly—that I loved!
If I could drench thy golden locks with tears,
What were it to this angel?

Gabriel. What love is!
And now I have named God.

Lucifer. Yet Gabriel,
By the lie in me which I keep myself,
Thou 'rt a false swearer. Were it otherwise,
What dost thou here, vouchsafing tender thoughts
To that earth-angel or earth-demon—which,
Thou and I have not solved his problem yet
Enough to argue,—that fallen Adam there.—
That red-clay and a breath! who must, forsooth,
Live in a new apocalypse of sense,
With beauty and music waving in his trees
And running in his rivers, to make glad
His soul made perfect; if it were not for
The hope within thee, deeper than thy truth,
Of finally conducting him and his
To fill the vacant thrones of me and mine,
Which affront Heaven with their vacuity?

Gabriel. Angel, there are no vacant thrones in Heaven
To suit thy bitter words. Glory and life
Fulfil their own depletions: and if God
Sighed you far from Him, His next breath drew in
A compensative splendor up the skies,

Flushing the starry arteries!
Lucifer. With a change!
So, let the vacant thrones, and gardens too,
Fill as may please you!—and be pitiful,
As ye translate that word, to the dethroned
And exiled, man or angel. The fact stands,
That I, the rebel, the cast out and down,
Am here, and will not go; while there, along
The light to which ye flash the desert out,
Flies your adopted Adam! your red clay
In two kinds, both being flawed. Why, what is this?
Whose work is this? Whose hand was in the work?
Against whose hand? In this last strife, methinks,
I am not a fallen angel!
Gabriel. Dost thou know
Aught of those exiles?
Lucifer. Ay: I know they have fled
Worldless all day along the wilderness:
I know they wear, for burden on their backs,
The thought of a shut gate of Paradise,
And faces of the marshalled cherubim
Shining against, not for them! and I know
They dare not look in one another's face,
As if each were a cherub!
Gabriel. Dost thou know
Aught of their future?
Lucifer. Only as much as this:
That evil will increase and multiply
Without a benediction.
Gabriel. Nothing more?

Lucifer. Why so the angels taunt! What should be more?

Gabriel. God is more.

Lucifer. Proving what?

Gabriel. That he is God,
And capable of saving. Lucifer,
I charge thee by the solitude He kept
Ere he created,—leave the earth to God!

Lucifer. My foot is on the earth, firm as my sin!

Gabriel. I charge thee by the memory of Heaven
Ere any sin was done,—leave earth to God!

Lucifer. My sin is on the earth, to reign thereon

Gabriel. I charge thee by the choral song we sang,
When up against the white shore of our feet,
The depths of the creation swelled and brake,—
And the new worlds, the beaded foam and flower
Of all that coil, roared outward into space
On thunder-edges,—leave the earth to God.

Lucifer. My woe is on the earth, to curse thereby.

Gabriel. I charge thee by that mournful morning star
Which trembles . . . . .

Lucifer. Hush! I will not hear thee speak
Of such things. Enough spoken. As the pine
In norland forest, drops its weight of snows
By a night's growth, so, growing toward my ends,
I drop thy counsels. Farewell, Gabriel!
Watch out thy service; I assert my will.
And peradventure in the after years,
When thoughtful men bend slow their spacious brows
Upon the storm and strife seen everywhere

To ruffle their smooth manhood, and break up
With lurid lights of intermittent hope
Their human fear and wrong,—they may discern
The heart of a lost angel in the earth.

CHORUS OF EDEN SPIRITS,

(Chanting from Paradise, while Adam and Eve fly across the sword-glare.)

Harken, oh harken! let your souls, behind you,
Lean, gently moved!
Our voices feel along the Dread to find you,
O lost, beloved!
Through the thick-shielded and strong-marshalled angels,
They press and pierce:
Our requiems follow fast on our evangels,—
Voice throbs in verse!
We are but orphaned Spirits left in Eden,
A time ago—
God gave us golden cups; and we were bidden
To feed you so!
But now our right hand hath no cup remaining,
No work to do;
The mystic hydromel is spilt, and staining
The whole earth through;
And all those stains lie clearly round for showing
(Not interfused!)
That brighter colors were the world's foregoing,
Than shall be used.
Harken, oh harken! ye shall harken surely,
For years and years,

The noise beside you, dripping coldly, purely,
Of spirits' tears!
The yearning to a beautiful, denied you,
Shall strain your powers:—
Ideal sweetnesses shall over-glide you,
Resumed from ours!
In all your music, our pathetic minor
Your ears shall cross;
And all fair sights shall mind you of diviner,
With sense of loss!
We shall be near, in all your poet-languors
And wild extremes;
What time ye vex the desert with vain angers,
Or light with dreams!
And when upon you, weary after roaming,
Death's seal is put,
By the forgone ye shall discern the coming,
Through eyelids shut.

Spirits of the trees.

Hark! the Eden trees are stirring,
Slow and solemn to your hearing!
Plane and cedar, palm and fir,
Tamarisk and juniper,
Each is throbbing in vibration
Since that crowning of creation,
When the God-breath spake abroad,
Pealing down the depths of Godhead
Let us make man like to God!
And the pine stood quivering
In the Eden-gorges wooded,
As the awful word went by;

Like a vibrant chorded string
Stretched from mountain-peak to sky!
And the platan did expand,
Slow and gradual, branch and head;
And the cedar's strong black shade
Fluttered brokenly and grand!—
Grove and forest bowed aslant
In emotion jubilant.

Voice of the same, but softer.

Which divine impulsion cleaves
In dim movements to the leaves
Dropt and lifted, dropt and lifted
In the sunlight greenly sifted,—
In the sunlight and the moonlight
Greenly sifted through the trees.
Ever wave the Eden trees
In the nightlight, and the noonlight,
With a ruffling of green branches
Shaded off to resonances;
Never stirred by rain or breeze!
Fare ye well, farewell!
The sylvan sounds, no longer audible,
Expire at Eden's door!
Each footstep of your treading
Treads out some murmur which ye heard before:
Farewell! the trees of Eden
Ye shall hear nevermore.

River-Spirits.

Hark! the flow of the four rivers—
Hark the flow!
How the silence round you shivers,

While our voices through it go,
Cold and clear.

A softer voice.

Think a little, while ye hear,—
Of the banks
Where the alders and red deer
Crowd in intermingled ranks,
As if all would drink at once,
Where the living water runs!
Of the fishes' golden edges
Flashing in and out the sedges:
Of the swans on silver thrones,
Floating down the winding streams,
With impassive eyes turned shoreward,
And a chant of undertones,—
And the lotos leaning forward
To help them into dreams.
Fare ye well, farewell!
The river-sounds, no longer audible,
Expire at Eden's door!
Each footstep of your treading
Treads out some murmur which ye heard before:
Farewell! the streams of Eden,
Ye shall hear nevermore.

Bird-Spirit.

I am the nearest nightingale
That singeth in Eden after you;
And I am singing loud and true,
And sweet,—I do not fail!
I sit upon a cypress-bough,
Close to the gate; and I fling my song

Over the gate and through the mail
Of the warden angels marshalled strong,—
Over the gate and after you!
And the warden angels let it pass,
Because the poor brown bird, alas!
Sings in the garden sweet and true.
And I build my song of high pure notes,
Note over note, height over height,
Till I strike the arch of the Infinite;
And I bridge abysmal agonies
With strong, clear calms of harmonies,—
And something abides, and something floats,
In the song which I sing after you:
Fare ye well, farewell!
The creature-sounds, no longer audible,
Expire at Eden's door!
Each footstep of your treading
Treads out some cadence which ye heard before:
Farewell! the birds of Eden
Ye shall hear nevermore.

Flower-Spirits.

We linger, we linger,
The last of the throng!
Like the tones of a singer
Who loves his own song
We are spirit-aromas
Of blossom and bloom;
We call your thoughts home, as
Ye breathe our perfume;
To the amaranth's splendor
Afire on the slopes;

To the lily-bells tender,
And grey heliotropes!
To the poppy-plains, keeping
Such dream-breath and blé,
That the angels there stepping
Grew whiter to see!
To the nook, set with moly,
Ye jested one day in,
Till your smile waxed too holy,
And left your lips praying!
To the rose in the bower-place,
That dripped o'er you sleeping;
To the asphodel flower place,
Ye walked ankle deep in!
We pluck at your raiment,
We stroke down your hair,—
We faint in our lament,
And pine into air.
Fare ye well, farewell!
The Eden scents, no longer sensible,
Expire at Eden's door!
Each footstep of your treading
Treads out some fragrance which ye knew before:
Farewell! the flowers of Eden,
Ye shall smell nevermore.

There is silence. ADAM *and* EVE *fly on, and never look back. Only a colossal shadow, as of the dark* ANGEL *passing quickly, is cast upon the sword-glare.*

SCENE.—*The extremity of the Sword-glare.*

Adam. Pausing a moment on this outer edge,
Where the supernal sword-glare cuts in light
The dark exterior desert,—hast thou strength,
Beloved, to look behind us to the gate?

Eve. Have I not strength to look up to thy face.

Adam. We need be strong: yon spectacle of cloud
Which seals the gate up to the final doom,
Is God's seal manifest. There seem to lie
A hundred thunders in it, dark and dead;
The unmolten lightnings vein it motionless;
And, outward from its depth, the self-moved sword
Swings slow its awful gnomon of red fire
From side to side,—in pendulous horror slow,—
Across the stagnant, ghastly glare thrown flat
On the intermediate ground from that to this,
In still reflection of still splendor. They,
The angelic hosts, the archangelic pomps,
Thrones, dominations, princedoms, rank on rank,
Rising sublimely to the feet of God,
On either side, and overhead the gate,—
Show like a glittering and sustained smoke
Drawn to an apex. That their faces shine
Betwixt the solemn claspings of their wings,
Clasped high to a silver point above their heads,—
We only guess from hence, and not discern.

Eve. Though we were near enough to see them shine,
The shadow on thy face were awfuller,

To me, at least,—than could appear their light.
Adam. What is this, Eve? thou droppest heavily
In a heap earthward; and thy body heaves
Under the golden floodings of thy hair!
Eve. O Adam, Adam! by that name of Eve—
Thine Eve, thy life—which suits me little now,
Seeing that I confess myself thy death
And thine undoer, as the snake was mine,—
I do adjure thee, put me straight away,
Together with my name. Sweet, punish me!
O Love, be just! and, ere we pass beyond
The light cast outward by the fiery sword,
Into the dark which earth must be to us,
Bruise my head with thy foot,—as the curse said
My seed shall the first tempter's: strike with curse,
As God struck in the garden! and as HE,
Being satisfied with justice and with wrath,
Did roll His thunder gentler at the close,—
Thou, peradventure, may'st at last recoil
To some soft need of mercy. Strike, my lord!
I, also, after tempting, writhe on ground;
And I would feed on ashes from thy hand,
As suits me, O my tempted.
Adam. My beloved,
Mine Eve and life—I have no other name
For thee or for the sun than what ye are,
My blessed life and light! If we have fallen,
It is that we have sinned,—we: God is just;
And since his curse doth comprehend us both,
It must be that His balance holds the weights
Of first and last sin on a level. What!

Shall I who had not virtue to stand straight
Among the hills of Eden, here assume
To mend the justice of the perfect God,
By piling up a curse upon His curse,
Against thee—thee—

Eve. For so, perchance, thy God
Might take thee into grace for scorning me;
Thy wrath against the sinner giving proof
Of inward abrogation of the sin!
And so, the blessed angels might come down
And walk with thee as erst,—I think they would,—
Because I was not near to make them sad,
Or soil the rustling of their innocence.

Adam. They know me. I am deepest in the guilt
If last in the transgression.

Eve. THOU!

Adam. If God!
Who gave the right and joyaunce of the world
Both unto thee and me,—gave thee to me,
The best gift last; the last sin was the worst,
Which sinned against more complement of gifts
And grace of giving. God! I render back
Strong benediction and perpetual praise
From mortal feeble lips, (as incense-smoke,
Out of a little censer, may fill heaven,)
That Thou, in striking my benumbed hands,
And forcing them to drop all other boons
Of beauty, and dominion, and delight,—
Hast left this well-beloved Eve—this life
Within life—this best gift between their palms,
In gracious compensation!

Eve Is it thy voice?
Or some saluting angel's—calling home
My feet into the garden?
Adam. O my God!
I, standing here between the glory and dark,—
The glory of thy wrath projected forth
From Eden's wall; the dark of our distress,
Which settles a step off in that drear world—
Lift up to Thee the hands from whence hath fallen
Only creation's sceptre,—thanking Thee
That rather Thou hast cast me out with *her*,
Than left me lorn of her in Paradise;—
With angel looks and angel songs around,
To show the absence of her eyes and voice,
And make society full desertness,
Without the uses of her comforting.
Eve. Or is it but a dream of thee, that speaks
Mine own love's tongue?
Adam. Because with *her*, I stand
Upright, as far as can be in this fall,
And look away from heaven, which doth accuse me,
And look away from earth which doth convict me,
Into her face; and crown my discrowned brow
Out of her love; and put the thought of her
Around me, for an Eden full of birds;
And lift her body up—thus—to my heart;
And with my lips upon her lips,—thus, thus,—
Do quicken and sublimate my mortal breath,
Which cannot climb against the grave's steep sides,
But overtops this grief!
Eve. I am renewed:

My eyes grow with the light which is in thine;
The silence of my heart is full of sound.
Hold me up—so! Because I comprehend
This human love, I shall not be afraid
Of any human death; and yet because
I know this strength of love, I seem to know
Death's strength, by that same sign. Kiss on my lips
To shut the door close on my rising soul,—
Lest it pass outwards in astonishment,
And leave thee lonely.

Adam. Yet thou liest, Eve,
Bent heavily on thyself across mine arm,
Thy face flat to the sky.

Eve. Ay! and the tears
Running as it might seem, my life from me;
They run so fast and warm. Let me lie so,
And weep so,—as if in a dream or prayer,—
Unfastening, clasp by clasp, the hard, tight thought
Which clipped my heart, and showed me evermore
Loathed of thy justice as I loathe the snake,
And as the pure ones loathe our sin. To-day,
All day, beloved, as we fled across
This desolating radiance, cast by swords
Not suns, my lips prayed soundless to myself,
Rocking against each other—O Lord God!
('Twas so I prayed) I ask Thee by my sin,
And by thy curse, and by thy blameless heavens,
Make dreadful haste to hide me from thy face,
And from the face of my beloved here,
For whom I am no helpmete, quick away
Into the new dark mystery of death!

I will lie still there ; I will make no plaint ;
I will not sigh, nor sob, nor speak a word,—
Nor struggle to come back beneath the sun,
Where peradventure I might sin anew
Against thy mercy and his pleasure. Death,
Oh, death, whate'er it be, is good enough
For such as I.—For Adam—there's no voice,
Shall ever say again, in heaven or earth,
It is not good for him to be alone.

Adam. And was it good for such a prayer to pass,
My unkind Eve, betwixt our mutual lives?
If I am exiled, must I be bereaved?

Eve. 'Twas an ill prayer: it shall be prayed no more;
And God did use it for a foolishness,
Giving no answer. Now my heart has grown
Too high and strong for such a foolish prayer:
Love makes it strong: and since I was the first
In the transgression, with a steady foot
I will be first to tread from this sword-glare
Into the outer darkness of the waste,—
And thus I do it.

Adam. Thus I follow thee,
As erewhile in the sin.—What sounds! what sounds!
I feel a music which comes slant from Heaven,
As tender as a watering dew.

Eve. I think
That angels—not those guarding Paradise,—
But the love-angels who came erst to us,
And when we said 'God,' fainted unawares
Back from our mortal presence unto God,

(As if He drew them inward in a breath)
His name being heard of them,—I think that they
With sliding voices lean from heavenly towers,
Invisible but gracious. Hark—how soft!

CHORUS OF INVISIBLE ANGELS.

(Faint and tender.)

Mortal man and woman,
  Go upon your travel!
Heaven assist the Human
  Smoothly to unravel
All that web of pain
  Wherein ye are holden.
Do ye know our voices
  Chanting down the golden?
Do ye guess our choice is,
  Being unbeholden,
To be harkened by you, yet again?
This pure door of opal,
  God hath shut between us;
Us, his shining people,—
  You who once have seen us,
And are blinded new!
  Yet across the doorway,
Past the silence reaching,
  Farewells evermore may,
Blessing in the teaching,
  Glide from us to you.

First semichorus.

Think how erst your Eden,
Day on day succeeding,

With our presence glowed.
We came as if the Heavens were bowed
To a milder music rare!
Ye saw us in our solemn treading,
Treading down the steps of cloud;
While our wings outspreading
Double calms of whiteness,
Dropped superfluous brightness
Down from stair to stair

Second semichorus.

Or, abrupt though tender,
While ye gazed on space,
We flashed our angel-splendor
In either human face!
With mystic lilies in our hands,
From the atmospheric bands,
Breaking, with a sudden grace,
We took you unaware!
While our feet struck glories
Outward, smooth and fair,
Which we stood on floorwise,
Platformed in mid air.

First Semichorus.

Oft when Heaven-descended,
Shut up in a secret light
Stood we speechless in your sight,
In a mute apocalypse!
With dumb vibrations on our lips,
From hosannas ended;
And grand half-vanishings
Of the foregone things,

Within our eyes belated!
Till the heavenly Infinite
Falling off from our Created,
Left our inward contemplation
Opening into ministration.

Chorus.

Then in odes of burning,
Brake we suddenly,
And sang out the morning
Broadly up the sky.—
Or we drew
Our music through
The noontide's hush and heat and shine,
And taught them our intense Divine—
With our vital fiery notes
All disparted hither, thither,
Trembling out into the æther,—
Visible like beamy motes!—
Or, as twilight drifted
Through the cedar masses.
The globed sun we lifted,
Trailing purple, trailing gold
Out between the passes
Of the mountains manifold,
To anthems slowly sung!
While he, aweary and in swoon,
For joy to hear our climbing tune
Pierce the faint stars' concentric rings,—
The burden of his glory flung
In broken lights upon our wings.

Chant dies away confusedly, and enter LUCIFER.

Lucifer. Now may all fruits be pleasant to thy lips,
Beautiful Eve! The times have somewhat changed
Since thou and I had talk beneath a tree;
Albeit ye are not gods yet.

Eve. Adam! hold
My right hand strongly. It is Lucifer—
And we have love to lose.

Adam. I' the name of God,
Go apart from us, O thou Lucifer!
And leave us to the desert thou hast made
Out of thy treason. Bring no serpent-slime
Athwart this path kept holy to our tears,
Or we may curse thee with their bitterness.

Lucifer. Curse freely! curses thicken. Why, this Eve
Who thought me once part worthy of her ear,
And somewhat wiser than the other beasts,—
Drawing together her large globes of eyes,
The light of which is throbbing in and out
Their steadfast continuity of gaze,—
Knots her fair eyebrows in so hard a knot,
And, down from her white heights of womanhood,
Looks on me so amazed,—I scarce should fear
To wager such an apple as she plucked,
Against one riper from the tree of life,
That she could curse too—as a woman may—
Smooth in the vowels.

Eve. So—speak wickedly!
I like it best so. Let thy words be wounds,—
For, so, I shall not fear thy power to hurt:
Trench on the forms of good by open ill—

For, so, I shall wax strong and grand with scorn;
Scorning myself for ever trusting thee
As far as thinking, ere a snake ate dust,
He could speak wisdom.

Lucifer. Our new gods, methinks,
Deal more in thunders than in courtesies:
And, sooth, mine own Olympus, which anon
I shall build up to loud-voiced imagery,
From all the wandering visions of the world,—
May show worse railing than our lady Eve
Pours o'er the rounding of her argent arm.
But why should this be? Adam pardoned Eve.

Adam. Adam loved Eve. Jehovah pardon both!

Eve. Adam forgave Eve—because loving Eve.

Lucifer. So, well. Yet Adam was undone of Eve,
As both were by the snake. Therefore forgive,
In like wise, fellow-temptress, the poor snake—
Who stung there, not so poorly! [*Aside.*

Eve. Hold thy wrath,
Beloved Adam! let me answer him;
For this time he speaks truth, which we should hear,
And asks for mercy, which I most should grant,
In like wise, as he tells us—in like wise!
And therefore I thee pardon, Lucifer,
As freely as the streams of Eden flowed,
When we were happy by them. So, depart;
Leave us to walk the remnant of our time
Out mildly in the desert. Do not seek
To harm us any more or scoff at us,
Or ere the dust be laid upon our face
To find there the communion of the dust

And issue of the curse.—Go.

Adam. At once, go.

Lucifer. Forgive! and go! Ye images of clay,
Shrunk somewhat in the mould,—what jest is this?
What words are these to use? By what a thought
Conceive ye of me? Yesterday—a snake!
To-day, what?

Adam. A strong spirit.

Eve. A sad spirit.

Adam. Perhaps a fallen angel.—Who shall say?

Lucifer. Who told thee, Adam?

Adam. *Thou!* The prodigy
Of thy vast brows and melancholy eyes,
Which comprehend the heights of some great fall.
I think that thou hast one day worn a crown
Under the eyes of God.

Lucifer. And why of God?

Adam. It were no crown else! Verily, I think
Thou 'rt fallen far. I had not yesterday
Said it so surely; but I know to-day
Grief by grief, sin by sin.

Lucifer. A crown by a crown.

Adam. Ay, mock me! now I know more than I knew.
Now I know thou art fallen below hope
Of final re-ascent.

Lucifer. Because?

Adam. Because
A spirit who expected to see God,
Though at the last point of a million years,
Could dare no mockery of a ruined man

Such as this Adam.

Lucifer. Who is high and bold—
Be it said passing!—of a good red clay
Discovered on some top of Lebanon,
Or haply of Aornus, beyond sweep
Of the black eagle's wing! A furlong lower
Had made a meeker king for Eden. Soh!
Is it not possible, by sin and grief
(To give the things your names) that spirits should rise
Instead of falling?

Adam. Most impossible.
The Highest being the Holy and the Glad,
Whoever rises must approach delight
And sanctity in the act.

Lucifer. Ha, my clay-king!
Thou wilt not rule by wisdom very long
The after generations. Earth, methinks,
Will disinherit thy philosophy
For a new doctrine suited to thine heirs;
Classing these present dogmas with the rest
Of the old-world traditions—Eden fruits
And saurian fossils.

Eve. Speak no more with him,
Beloved! it is not good to speak with him.
Go from us, Lucifer, and speak no more:
We have no pardon which thou dost not scorn,
Nor any bliss, thou seest, for coveting,
Nor innocence for staining. Being bereft,
We would be alone.—Go.

Lucifer. Ah! ye talk the same,
All of you—spirits and clay—go, and depart!

In Heaven they said so; and at Eden's gate,—
And here, reiterant, in the wilderness!
None saith, Stay with me, for thy face is fair!
None saith, Stay with me, for thy voice is sweet!
And yet I was not fashioned out of clay.
Look on me, woman! Am I beautiful?

Eve. Thou hast a glorious darkness.

Lucifer. Nothing more?

Eve. I think no more.

Lucifer. False Heart—thou thinkest more!
Thou canst not choose but think, as I praise God,
Unwillingly but fully, that I stand
Most absolute in beauty. As yourselves
Were fashioned very good at best, so *we*
Sprang very beauteous from the creant Word
Which thrilled around us—God Himself being moved,
When that august work of a perfect shape,
His dignities of sovran angel-hood,
Swept out into the universe,—divine
With thunderous movements, earnest looks of gods,
And silver-solemn clash of cymbal wings.
Whereof was I. in motion and in form,
A part not poorest. And yet,—yet, perhaps,
This beauty which I speak of, is not here,
As God's voice is not here; nor even my crown—
I do not know. What is this thought or thing
Which I call beauty? is it thought or thing?
Is it a thought accepted for a thing?
Or both? or neither?—a pretext?—a word?
Its meaning flutters in me like a flame
Under my own breath: my perceptions reel

For evermore around it, and fall off,
As if it too were holy.
Eve. Which it is.
Adam. The essence of all beauty I call love.
The attribute, the evidence, and end,
The consummation to the inward sense,
Of beauty apprehended from without,
I still call love. As form, when colorless,
Is nothing to the eye; that pine tree there,
Without its black and green, being all a blank;
So, without love, is beauty undiscerned
In man or angel. Angel! rather ask
What love is in thee, what love moves to thee,
And what collateral love moves on with thee;
Then shalt thou know if thou art beautiful.
Lucifer. Love! what is love? I lose it. Beauty and love!
I darken to the image. Beauty—Love!
[*He fades away, while a low music sounds.*
Adam. Thou art pale, Eve.
Eve. The precipice of ill
Down this colossal nature, dizzies me—
And, hark! the starry harmony remote
Seems measuring the heights from whence he fell.
Adam. Think that we have not fallen so. By the hope
And aspiration, by the love and faith,
We do exceed the stature of this angel.
Eve. Happier we are than he is, by the death!
Adam. Or rather, by the life of the Lord God!
How dim the angel grows, as if that blast

Of music swept him back into the dark.

[*The music is stronger, gathering itself into uncertain articulation.*

Eve. It throbs in on us like a plaintive heart,
Pressing, with slow pulsations, vibrative.
Its gradual sweetness through the yielding air,
To such expression as the stars may use,
Most starry-sweet, and strange! With every note
That grows more loud, the angel grows more dim,
Receding in proportion to approach,
Until he stand afar,—a shade.

Adam. Now, words.

SONG OF THE MORNING STAR TO LUCIFER.

He fades utterly away and vanishes, as it proceeds.

Mine orbed image sinks
Back from thee, back from thee,
As thou art fallen, methinks,
Back from me, back from me.
O my light-bearer,
Could another fairer
Lack to thee, lack to thee?
Ai, ai, Heosphoros!
I loved thee, with the fiery love of stars,
Who love by burning, and by loving move,
Too near the throned Jehovah, not to love.
Ai, ai, Heosphoros!
Their brows flash fast on me from gliding cars,
Pale-passioned for my loss.
Ai, ai, Heosphoros!

Mine orbed heats drop cold
Down from thee, down from thee,

As fell thy grace of old
Down from me, down from me.
O my light-bearer,
Is another fairer
Won to thee, won to thee?
Ai, ai, Heosphoros,
Great love preceded loss,
Known to thee, known to thee.
Ai, ai!
Thou, breathing thy cummunicable grace
Of life into my light,
Mine astral faces, from thine angel face,
Hast inly fed,
And flooded me with radiance overmuch
From thy pure height.
Ai, ai!
Thou, with calm, floating pinions both ways spread,
Erect, irradiated,
Didst sting my wheel of glory
On, on before thee,
Along the Godlight, by a quickening touch!
Ha, ha!
Around, around the firmamental ocean,
I swam expanding with delirious fire!
Around, around, around, in blind desire
To be drawn upward to the Infinite—
Ha, ha!

Until, the motion flinging out the motion
To a keen whirl of passion and avidity,—
To a blind whirl of rapture and delight,—

I wound in girant orbits, smooth and white
With that intense rapidity!
Around, around,
I wound and interwound,
While all the cyclic heavens about me spun!
Stars, planets, suns, and moons, dilated broad,
Then flashed together into a single sun,
And wound, and wound in one;
And as they wound I wound,—around, around,
In a great fire, I almost took for God!
Ha, ha, Heosphoros!

Thine angel glory sinks
Down from me, down from me—
My beauty falls, methinks,
Down from thee, down from thee!
O my light-bearer,
O my path-preparer,
Gone from me, gone from me!
Ai, ai, Heosphoros!
I cannot kindle underneath the brow
Of this new angel here, who is not Thou:
All things are altered since that time ago,—
And if I shine at eve, I shall not know—
I am strange—I am slow!
Ai, ai, Heosophoros!
Henceforward, human eyes of lovers be
The only sweetest sight that I shall see,
With tears between the looks raised up to me.
Ai, ai!
When, having wept all night, at break of day,

Above the folded hills they shall survey
My light, a little trembling, in the grey,
Ai, ai!
And gazing on me, such shall comprehend,
Through all my piteous pomp at morn or even,
And melancholy leaning out of Heaven,
That love, their own divine, may change or end,
That love may close in loss!
Ai, ai, Heosphoros!

SCENE.—*Farther on. A wild open country seen vaguely in the approaching night.*

Adam. How doth the wide and melancholy earth
Gather her hills around us, grey and ghast,
And stare with blank significance of loss
Right in our faces! Is the wind up?

Eve. Nay.

Adam. And yet the cedars and the junipers
Rock slowly through the mist, without a sound;
And shapes, which have no certainty of shape,
Drift duskly in and out between the pines,
And loom along the edges of the hills,
And lie flat, curdling in the open ground—
Shadows without a body, which contract
And lengthen as we gaze on them.

Eve. O Life
Which is not man's nor angel's! What is this?

Adam. No cause for fear. The circle of God's life
Contains all life beside.

Eve I think the earth
Is crazed with curse, and wanders from the sense

Of those first laws affixed to form and space
Or ever she knew sin!

Adam. We will not fear:
We were brave sinning.

Eve. Yea, I plucked the fruit
With eyes upturned to Heaven, and seeing there
Our god-thrones, as the tempter said—not GOD.
My heart, which beat then, sinks. The sun hath sunk
Out of sight with our Eden.

Adam. Night is near.

Eve. And God's curse, nearest. Let us travel back,
And stand within the sword-glare till we die;
Believing it is better to meet death
Than suffer desolation.

Adam. Nay, beloved!
We must not pluck death from the Maker's hand,
As erst we plucked the apple: we must wait
Until He gives death, as He gave us life;
Nor murmur faintly o'er the primal gift,
Because we spoilt its sweetness with our sin.

Eve. Ah, ah! Dost thou discern what I behold?

Adam. I see all. How the spirits in thine eyes,
From their dilated orbits, bound before
To meet the spectral Dread!

Eve. I am afraid—
Ah, ah! The twilight bristles wild with shapes
Of intermittent motion, aspect vague
And mystic bearings, which o'ercreep the earth,
Keeping slow time with horrors in the blood.
How near they reach . . . and far! how gray they move—

Treading upon the darkness without feet,—
And fluttering on the darkness without wings!
Some run like dogs, with noses to the ground;
Some keep one path, like sheep; some rock like trees
Some glide like a fallen leaf; and some flow on,
Copious as rivers.

Adam. Some spring up like fire—
And some coil . . .

Eve. Ah, ah! Dost thou pause to say
Like what?—coil like the serpent when he fell
From all the emerald splendor of his height,
And writhed,—and could not climb against the curse,
Not a ring's length. I am afraid—afraid—
I think it is God's will to make me afraid,
Permitting THESE to haunt us in the place
Of His beloved angels—gone from us,
Because we are not pure. Dear Pity of God,
That didst permit the angels to go home,
And live no more with us who are not pure;
Save *us* too from a loathly company—
Almost as loathly in our eyes, perhaps,
As *we* are in the purest! Pity us—
Us too! nor shut us in the dark, away
From verity and from stability,
Or what we name such, through the precedence
Of earth's adjusted uses,—evermore
To doubt, betwixt our senses and our souls,
Which are the most distraught, and full of pain,
And weak of apprehension.

Adam. Courage, sweet!
The mystic shapes ebb back from us, and drop

With slow concentric movement, each on each,—
Expressing wider spaces, and collapsed
In lines more definite for imagery
And clearer for relation; till the throng
Of shapeless spectra merge into a few
Distinguishable phantasms, vague and grand,
Which sweep out and around us vastily,
And hold us in a circle and a calm.

Eve. Strange phantasms of pale shadow! there are twelve.
Thou, who didst name all lives, hast names for these?

Adam. Methinks this is the zodiac of the earth,
Which rounds us with its visionary dread,—
Responding with twelve shadowy signs of earth,
In fantasque apposition and approach,
To those celestial, constellated twelve
Which palpitate adown the silent nights
Under the pressure of the hand of God,
Stretched wide in benediction. At this hour,
Not a star pricketh the flat gloom of heaven!
But, girdling close our nether wilderness,
The zodiac-figures of the earth loom slow,—
Drawn out, as suiteth with the place and time,
In twelve colossal shades, instead of stars,
Through which the ecliptic line of mystery
Strikes bleakly with an unrelenting scope,
Foreshowing life and death.

Eve. By dream or sense,
Do we see this?

Adam. Our spirits have climbed high
By reason of the passion of our grief,—

And from the top of sense, looked over sense,
To the significance and heart of things
Rather than things themselves.
Eve. And the dim twelve . . .
Adam. Are dim exponents of the creature-life
As earth contains it. Gaze on them, beloved!
By stricter apprehension of the sight,
Suggestions of the creatures shall assuage
Thy terror of the shadows;—what is known
Subduing the unknown, and taming it
From all prodigious dread. That phantasm, there,
Presents a lion,—albeit, twenty times
As large as any lion —with a roar
Set soundless in his vibratory jaws,
And a strange horror stirring in his mane!
And, there, a pendulous shadow seems to weigh—
Good against ill, perchance; and there, a crab
Puts coldly out its gradual shadow-claws,
Like a slow blot that spreads,—till all the ground,
Crawled over by it, seems to crawl itself;
A bull stands horned here with gibbous glooms;
And a ram likewise; and a scorpion writhes
Its tail in ghastly slime, and stings the dark!
This way a goat leaps, with wild blank of beard;
And here fantastic fishes duskly float,
Using the calm for waters, while their fins
Throb out slow rhythms along the shallow air!
While images more human——
Eve. How he stands,
That phantasm of a man—who is not *thou!*
Two phantasms of two men.

Adam. One that sustains,
And one that strives!—resuming, so, the ends
Of manhood's curse of labor.* Dost thou see
That phantasm of a woman?—
Eve. I have seen—
But look off to those small humanities,†
Which draw me tenderly across my fear,—
Lesser and fainter than my womanhood,
Or yet thy manhood—with strange innocence
Set in the misty lines of head and hand
They lean together! I would gaze on them
Longer and longer, till my watching eyes,—
As the stars do in watching anything,—
Should light them forward from their outline vague,
To clear configuration—

Two Spirits, of organic and inorganic nature, arise from the ground.

But what Shapes
Rise up between us in the open space,—
And thrust me into horror, back from hope?
Adam. Colossal Shapes—twin sovran images,—
With a disconsolate, blank majesty
Set in their wondrous faces!—with no look,
And yet an aspect—a significance
Of individual life and passionate ends,
Which overcomes us gazing.

---

* Adam recognizes in *Aquarius*, the water-bearer, and *Sagittarius*, the archer, distinct types of the man bearing and the man combatting,—the passive and active forms of human labor. I hope that the preceding zodiacal signs—transferred to the earthly shadow and representative purpose—of Aries, Taurus, Cancer, Leo, Libra, Scorpio, Capricornus, and Pisces, are sufficiently obvious to the reader.

† Her maternal instinct is excited by *Gemini*.

O bleak sound!
O shadow of sound, O phantasm of thin sound!
How it comes, wheeling as the pale moth wheels,
Wheeling and wheeling in continuous wail,
Around the cyclic zodiac; and gains force,
And gathers, settling coldly like a moth,
On the wan faces of these images
We see before us; whereby modified
It draws a straight line of articulate song
From out that spiral faintness of lament—
And, by one voice, expresses many griefs.

First Spirit.

I am the spirit of the harmless earth;
God spake me softly out among the stars,
As softly as a blessing of much worth,—
And then, His smile did follow unawares,
That all things, fashioned, so, for use and duty,
Might shine anointed with His chrism of beauty—
Yet I wail!
I drave on with the worlds exultingly,
Obliquely down the Godlight's gradual fall—
Individual aspect and complexity
Of gyratory orb and interval,
Lost in the fluent motion of delight
Toward the high ends of Being, beyond sight—
Yet I wail!

Second Spirit.

I am the Spirit of the harmless beasts,
Of flying things, and creeping things, and swimming;
Of all the lives, erst set at silent feasts,
That found the love-kiss on the goblet brimming,

And tasted, in each drop within the measure,
The sweetest pleasure of their Lord's good pleasure—
Yet I wail!
What a full hum of life, around His lips,
Bore witness to the fulness of creation!
How all the grand words were full-laden ships;
Each sailing onward, from enunciation,
To separate existence,—and each bearing
The creature's power of joying, hoping, fearing!—
Yet I wail!

Eve. They wail, beloved! they speak of glory and God,
And they wail—wail. That burden of the song
Drops from it like its fruit, and heavily falls
Into the lap of silence!

Adam. Hark, again!

First Spirit

I was so beautiful, so beautiful,
My joy stood up within me bold and glad,
To answer God; and when His work was full,
To "very good," responded "very glad!"
Filtered through roses, did the light enclose me;
And bunches of the grape swam blue across me—
Yet I wail!

Second Spirit.

I bounded with my panthers! I rejoiced
In my young tumbling lions, rolled together!
My stag—the river at his fetlocks—poised,
Then dipped his antlers, through the golden weather,
In the same ripple which the alligator
Left in his joyous troubling of the water—

Yet I wail!

First Spirit.

O my deep waters, cataract and flood,—
What wordless triumph did your voices render!
O mountain-summits, where the angels stood,
And shook from head and wing thick dews of
splendor;
How with a holy quiet, did your Earthy
Accept that Heavenly—knowing ye were worthy!
Yet I wail!

Second Spirit.

O my wild wood dogs, with your listening eyes!
My horses—my ground eagles, for swift fleeing!
My birds, with viewless wings of harmonies,—
My calm cold fishes of a silver being,—
How happy were ye, living and possessing,
O fair half-souls, capacious of full blessing.
Yet I wail!

First Spirit.

I wail, I wail! Now hear my charge to-day,
Thou man, thou woman, marked as the misdoers,
By God's sword at your backs! I lent my clay
To make your bodies, which had grown more flowers:
And now, in change for what I lent, ye give me
The thorn to vex, the tempest-fire to cleave me—
And I wail!

Second Spirit.

I wail, I wail! Behold ye that I fasten
My sorrow's fang upon your souls dishonored?
Accursed transgressors! down the steep ye hasten,—

Your crown's weight on the world, to drag it downward
Unto your ruin. Lo! my lions, scenting
The blood of wars, roar hoarse and unrelenting—
And I wail!

First Spirit.
I wail, I wail! Do ye hear that I wail?
I had no part in your transgression—none!
My roses on the bough did bud not pale—
My rivers did not loiter in the sun.
I was obedient. Wherefore, in my centre,
Do I thrill at this curse of death and winter!—
And I wail!

Second Spirit.
I wail, I wail! I shriek in the assault
Of undeserved perdition, sorely wounded!
My nightingales sang sweet without a fault,
My gentle leopards innocently bounded;
We were obedient—what is this convulses
Our blameless life with pangs and fever pulses?
And I wail!

Eve. I choose God's thunder and His angels' swords
To die by, Adam, rather than such words.
Let us pass out, and flee.

Adam. We cannot flee.
This zodiac of the creatures' cruelty
Curls round us, like a river cold and drear,
And shuts us in, constraining us to hear.

First Spirit.
I feel your steps, O wandering sinners, strike
A sense of death to me, and undug graves!

The heart of earth, once calm, is trembling, like
  The ragged foam along the ocean-waves:
The restless earthquakes rock against each other;—
The elements moan 'round me—"Mother, mother"—
          And I wail!

Second Spirit.

Your melancholy looks do pierce me through;
  Corruption swathes the paleness of your beauty.
Why have ye done this thing? What did we do
  That we should fall from bliss, as ye from duty?
Wild shriek the hawks, in waiting for their jesses,
Fierce howl the wolves along the wildernesses—
          And I wail!

Adam. To thee, the Spirit of the harmless earth—
To thee, the Spirit of earth's harmless lives—
Inferior creatures, but still innocent—
Be salutation from a guilty mouth,
Yet worthy of some audience and respect
From you who are not guilty. If we have sinned,
God hath rebuked us, who is over us,
To give rebuke or death; and if ye wail
Because of any suffering from our sin,
Ye, who are under and not over us,
Be satisfied with God, if not with us,
And pass out from our presence in such peace
As we have left you, to enjoy revenge,
Such as the Heavens have made you. Verily,
There must be strife between us, large as sin.

Eve. No strife, mine Adam! Let us not stand high
Upon the wrong we did, to reach disdain,
Who rather should be humbler evermore,

Since self-made sadder. Adam! shall I speak—
I who spake once to such a bitter end—
Shall I speak humbly now, who once was proud?
I, schooled by sin to more humility
Than thou hast, O mine Adam, O my king—
My king, if not the world's?

Adam. Speak as thou wilt.

Eve. Thus then—my hand in thine—
. . . . Sweet, dreadful Spirits!
I pray you humbly in the name of God;
Not to say of these tears, which are impure—
Grant me such pardoning grace as can go forth
From clean volitions toward a spotted will,
From the wronged to the wronger; this and no more;
I do not ask more. I am 'ware, indeed,
That absolute pardon is impossible
From you to me, by reason of my sin,—
And that I cannot evermore, as once,
With worthy acceptation of pure joy,
Behold the trances of the holy hills
Beneath the leaning stars; or watch the vales,
Dew-pallid with their morning ecstasy;
Or hear the winds make pastoral peace between
Two grassy uplands,—and the river-wells
Work out their bubbling lengths beneath the ground—
And all the birds sing, till, for joy of song,
They lift their trembling wings, as if to heave
The too-much weight of music from their heart
And float it up the æther! I am 'ware
That these things I can no more apprehend,
With a pure organ, into a full delight;

The sense of beauty and of melody
Being no more aided in me by the sense
Of personal adjustment to those heights
Of what I see well-formed or hear well-tuned,—
But rather coupled darkly, and made ashamed,
By my percipiency of sin and fall,
And melancholy of humiliant thoughts.
But, oh! fair, dreadful Spirits—albeit this
Your accusation must confront my soul,
And your pathetic utterance and full gaze
Must evermore subdue me; be content—
Conquer me gently—as if pitying me,
Not to say loving! let my tears fall thick
As watering dews of Eden, unreproached;
And when your tongues reprove me, make me smooth,
Not ruffled—smooth and still with your reproof,
And peradventure better, while more sad.
For look to it, sweet Spirits—look well to it—
It will not be amiss in you who kept
The law of your own righteousness, and keep
The right of your own griefs to mourn themselves,—
To pity me twice fallen,—from that, and this,—
From joy of place, and also right of wail,—
"I wail" being not for me—only "I sin."
Look to it, O sweet Spirits!—

For was I not,
At that last sunset seen in Paradise,
When all the westering clouds flashed out in throngs
Of sudden angel-faces, face by face,
All hushed and solemn, as a thought of God
Held them suspended,—was I not, that hour,

The lady of the world, princess of life,
Mistress of feast and favor? Could I touch
A rose with my white hand, but it became
Redder at once? Could I walk leisurely
Along our swarded garden, but the grass
Tracked me with greenness? Could I stand aside
A moment underneath a cornel-tree,
But all the leaves did tremble as alive,
With songs of fifty birds who were made glad
Because I stood there? Could I turn to look
With these twain eyes of mine, now weeping fast,
Now good for only weeping—upon man,
Angel, or beast, or bird, but each rejoiced
Because I looked on him? Alas, alas!
And is not this much wo, to cry "alas!"
Speaking of joy? And is not this more shame,
To have made the wo myself, from all that joy?
To have stretched my hand, and plucked it from the tree,
And chosen it for fruit? Nay, is not this
Still most despair,—to have halved that bitter fruit,
And ruined, so, the sweetest friend I have,
Turning the GREATEST to mine enemy?

Adam. I will not hear thee speak so. Hearken, Spirits!
Our God, who is the enemy of none,
But only of their sin,—hath set your hope
And my hope, in a promise, on this Head.
Show reverence, then,—and never bruise her more
With unpermitted and extreme reproach;
Lest, passionate in anguish, she fling down

Beneath your trampling feet, God's gift to us,
Of sovranty by reason and freewill;
Sinning against the province of the Soul
To rule the soulless. Reverence her estate:
And pass out from her presence with no words.

Eve. O dearest Heart, have patience with my heart,—
O Spirits, have patience, 'stead of reverence,—
And let me speak; for, not being innocent,
It little doth become me to be proud;
And I am prescient by the very hope
And promise set upon me, that henceforth,
Only my gentleness shall make me great,
My humbleness exalt me. Awful Spirits,
Be witness that I stand in your reproof
But one sun's length off from my happiness—
Happy, as I have said, to look around—
Clear to look up!—And now! I need not speak—
Ye see me what I am; ye scorn me so,—
Because ye see me what I have made myself
From God's best making! Alas,—peace forgone,—
Love wronged,—and virtue forfeit, and tears wept
Upon all, vainly! Alas, me! alas,
Who have undone myself from all that best,
Fairest and sweetest, to this wretchedest,
Saddest and most defiled—cast out, cast down—
What word metes absolute loss? let absolute loss
Suffice you for revenge. For *I*, who lived
Beneath the wings of angels yesterday,
Wander to-day beneath the roofless world!
I, reigning the earth's empress, yesterday,

Put off from me, to-day, your hate with prayers!
I, yesterday, who answered the Lord God,
Composed and glad, as singing-birds the sun,
Might shriek now from our dismal desert, "God,"
And hear Him make reply, "What is thy need,
Thou whom I cursed to-day?"

Adam. Eve!

Eve. *I*, at last,
Who yesterday was helpmate and delight
Unto mine Adam, am to-day the grief
And curse-mete for him! And, so, pity us,
Ye gentle Spirits, and pardon him and me,
And let some tender peace, made of our pain,
Grow up betwixt us, as a tree might grow
With boughs on both sides. In the shade of which,
When presently ye shall behold us dead,—
For the poor sake of our humility,
Breathe out your pardon on our breathless lips,
And drop your twilight dews against our brows;
And stroking with mild airs, our harmless hands
Left empty of all fruit, perceive your love
Distilling through your pity over us,
And suffer it, self-reconciled, to pass.

LUCIFER *rises in the circle.*

Lucifer. Who talks here of a complement of grief?
Of expiation wrought by loss and fall?
Of hate subduable to pity? Eve?
Take counsel from thy counsellor the snake,
And boast no more in grief, nor hope from pain,
My docile Eve! I teach you to despond,
Who taught you disobedience. Look around;—

Earth-spirits and phantasms hear you talk, unmoved,
As if ye were red clay again, and talked!
What are your words to them? your griefs to them?
Your deaths, indeed, to them? Did the hand pause
For *their* sake, in the plucking of the fruit,
That they should pause for *you*, in hating you?
Or will your grief or death, as did your sin,
Bring change upon their final doom? Behold,
Your grief is but your sin in the rebound,
And cannot expiate for it.

Adam. That is true.

Lucifer. Ay, it is true. The clay-king testifies
To the snake's counsel,—hear him!—very true.

Earth Spirits. I wail, I wail!

Lucifer. And certes, *that* is true.
Ye wail, ye all wail. Peradventure I
Could wail among you. O thou universe,
That holdest sin and wo,—more room for wail!

Distant starry voice. Ai, ai, Heosphoros!

Earth Spirits. I wail, I wail!

Adam. Mark Lucifer. He changes awfully.

Eve. It seems as if he looked from grief to God.
And could not see Him;—wretched Lucifer!

Adam. How he stands—yet an angel!

Earth Spirits. I wail—wail!

Lucifer. (*After a pause.*) Dost thou remember,
Adam, when the curse
Took us in Eden? On a mountain-peak
Half-sheathed in primal woods, and glittering
In spasms of awful sunshine, at that hour
A lion couched,—part raised upon his paws,

With his calm, massive face turned full on thine,
And his mane listening. When the ended curse
Left silence in the world,—right suddenly
He sprang up rampant, and stood straight and stiff,
As if the new reality of death
Were dashed against his eyes,—and roared so fierce
(Such thick carnivorous passion in his throat
Tearing a passage through the wrath and fear)—
And roared so wild, and smote from all the hills
Such fast, keen echoes crumbling down the vales
Precipitately,—that the forest beasts,
One after one, did mutter a response
In savage and in sorrowful complaint
Which trailed along the gorges. Then, at once,
He fell back, and rolled crashing from the height,
Hid by the dark-orbed pines.

Adam. It might have been.
I heard the curse alone.

Earth Spirits. I wail, I wail!

Lucifer. That lion is a type of what I am!
And as he fixed thee with his full-faced hate,
And roared, O Adam—comprehending doom;
So, gazing on the face of the Unseen,
I cry out here, between the heavens and earth,
My conscience of this sin, this wo, this wrath,
Which damn me to this depth!

Earth Spirits. I wail, I wail!

Eve. I wail—O God!

Lucifer. I scorn you that ye wail,
Who use your petty griefs for pedestals
To stand on, beckoning pity from without,

And deal in pathos of antithesis
Of what ye *were* forsooth, and what ye are ;—
I scorn you like an angel ! Yet, one cry,
I, too, would drive up, like a column erect,
Marble to marble, from my heart to Heaven,
A monument of anguish, to transpierce
And overtop your vapory complaints
Expressed from feeble woes !

Earth Spirits. I wail, I wail !

Lucifer. For, O ye heavens, ye are my witnesses,
That *I*, struck out from nature in a blot,
The outcast, and the mildew of things good,
The leper of angels, the excepted dust
Under the common rain of daily gifts,—
I the snake, I the tempter, I the cursed,—
To whom the highest and the lowest alike
Say, Go from us—we have no need of thee,—
Was made by God like others. Good and fair,
He did create me !—ask Him, if not fair ;
Ask, if I caught not fair and silverly
His blessing for chief angels, on my head,
Until it grew there, a crown crystallized !
Ask, if He never called me by my name,
Lucifer—kindly said as " Gabriel "—
Lucifer—soft as " Michael !" While serene
I, standing in the glory of the lamps,
Answered " my father," innocent of shame
And of the sense of thunder. Ha ! ye think,
White angels in your niches,—I repent,—
And would tread down my own offences, back
To service at the footstool ! *That's* read wrong:

I cry as the beast did, that I may cry—
Expansive, not appealing! Fallen so deep
Against the sides of this prodigious pit,
I cry—cry—dashing out the hands of wail,
On each side, to meet anguish everywhere,
And to attest it in the ecstasy
And exaltation of a wo sustained
Because provoked and chosen.
Pass along
Your wilderness, vain mortals! Puny griefs,
In transitory shapes, be henceforth dwarfed
To your own conscience, by the dread extremes
Of what I am and have been. If ye have fallen,
It is a step's fall,—the whole ground beneath
Strewn woolly soft with promise; if ye have sinned,
Your prayers tread high as angels! if ye have grieved,
Ye are too mortal to be pitiable,
The power to die disproves the right to grieve.
Go to! ye call this ruin. I half-scorn
The ill I did you! Were ye wronged by me,
Hated and tempted, and undone of me,—
Still, what's your hurt to mine, of doing hurt,
Of hating, tempting, and so ruining?
This sword's *hilt* is the sharpest, and cuts through
The hand that wields it.
Go—I curse you all.
Hate one another—feebly—as ye can;
I would not certes cut you short in hate—
Far be it from me! hate on as ye can!
I breathe into your faces, spirits of earth,
As wintry blast may breathe on wintry leaves,

And lifting up their brownness, show beneath
The branches very bare.—Beseech you, give
To Eve, who beggarly entreats your love
For her and Adam when they shall be dead,
An answer rather fitting to the sin
Than to the sorrow—as the Heavens, I trow,
For justice' sake gave theirs.

I curse you both,
Adam and Eve! Say grace as after meat,
After my curses. May your tears fall hot
On all the hissing scorns o' the creatures here,—
And yet rejoice. Increase and multiply,
Ye and your generations, in all plagues,
Corruptions, melancholies, poverties,
And hideous forms of life and fears of death;
The thought of death being alway eminent
Immoveable and dreadful in your life,
And deafly and dumbly insignificant
Of any hope beyond,—as death itself,—
Whichever of you lieth dead the first,—
Shall seem to the survivor—yet rejoice!
My curse catch at you strongly, body and soul,
And HE find no redemption—nor the wing
Of seraph move your way—and yet rejoice!
Rejoice,—because ye have not set in you
This hate which shall pursue you—this fire-hate
Which glares without, because it burns within—
Which kills from ashes—this potential hate,
Wherein I, angel, in antagonism
To God and his reflex beatitudes,
Moan ever in the central universe,

With the great wo of striving against Love—
And gasp for space amid the infinite—
And toss for rest amid the Desertness—
Self-orphaned by my will, and self-elect
To kingship of resistant agony
Toward the Good round me—hating good and love.
And willing to hate good and to hate love,
And willing to will on so evermore,
Scorning the Past, and damning the To come—
Go and rejoice ! I curse you !

LUCIFER *vanishes.*

Earth Spirits.

And we scorn you ! there's no pardon
Which can lean to you aright !
When your bodies take the guerdon
Of the death-curse in our sight,
Then the bee that hummeth lowest shall transcend you.
Then ye shall not move an eyelid
Though the stars look down your eyes ;
And the earth, which ye defiled,
She shall show you to the skies,—
" Lo ! these kings of ours—who sought to comprehend you."

First Spirit.

And the elements shall boldly
All your dust to dust constrain ;
Unresistedly and coldly,
I will smite you with my rain !
From the slowest of my frosts is no receding.

Second Spirit.

And my little worm, appointed

To assume a royal part,
He shall reign, crowned and anointed,
O'er the noble human heart!
Give him counsel against losing of that Eden!

Adam. Do ye scorn us? Back your scorn
Toward your faces gray and lorn,
As the wind drives back the rain,
Thus I drive with passion-strife;
I who stand beneath God's sun,
Made like God, and, though undone,
Not unmade for love and life.
Lo! ye utter words in vain!
By my free will that chose sin,
By mine agony within
Round the passage of the fire;
By the pinings which disclose
That my native soul is higher
Than what it chose,—
We are yet too high, O spirits, for your disdain.

Eve. Nay, beloved! if these be low,
We confront them with no height;
We stooped down to their level
In working them that evil;
And their scorn that meets our blow,
Scathes aright.
Amen. Let it be so.

Earth Spirits.

We shall triumph—triumph greatly,
When ye lie beneath the sward!
There, our lily shall grow stately,
Though ye answer not a word—

And her fragrance shall be scornful of your silence:
While your throne, ascending calmly,
We, in heirdom of your soul,
Flash the river, lift the palm tree,
The dilated ocean, roll
With the thoughts that throbbed within you—round the islands.

Alp and torrent shall inherit
Your significance of will:
With the grandeur of your spirit,
Shall our broad savannahs fill—
In our winds, your exultations shall be springing.
Even your parlance which inveigles,
By our rudeness shall be won;
Hearts poetic in our eagles,
Shall beat up against the sun,
And pour downward, in articulate clear singing.

Your bold speeches, our Behemoth,
With his thunderous jaw, shall wield!
Your high fancies shall our Mammoth
Breathe sublimely up the shield
Of St. Michael, at God's throne, who waits to speed him!
Till the heavens' smooth-grooved thunder
Spinning back, shall leave them clear;
And the angels, smiling wonder,
With dropt looks from sphere to sphere,
Shall cry, "Ho, ye heirs of Adam! ye exceed him!"

Adam. Root out thine eyes, sweet, from the dreary ground.
Beloved, we may be overcome by God,
But not by *these.*

Eve. By God, perhaps, in *these.*

Adam. I think, not so. Had God foredoomed despair,
He had not spoken hope. He may destroy,
Certes, but not deceive.

Eve. Behold this rose!
I plucked it in our bower of Paradise
This morning as I went forth; and my heart
Hath beat against its petals all the day.
I thought it would be always red and full,
As when I plucked it—*Is* it?—ye may see!
I cast it down to you that ye may see,
All of you!—count the petals lost of it—
And note the colors fainted! ye may see:
And I am as it is, who yesterday
Grew in the same place. O ye spirits of earth!
I almost, from my miserable heart,
Could here upbraid you for your cruel heart,
Which will not let me, down the slope of death,
Draw any of your pity after me,
Or lie still in the quiet of your looks,
As my flower, there, in mine.

[*A bleak wind, quickened with indistinct human voices, spins around the earth-zodiac; and filling the circle with its presence, and then wailing off into the east, carries the flower away with it.* EVE *falls upon her face.* ADAM *stands erect.*

Adam. So, verily,
The last departs.

Eve. So Memory follows Hope,
And Life both. Love said to me, "Do not die,"
And I replied, "O Love, I will not die.
I exiled and I will not orphan Love."
But now it is no choice of mine to die—
My heart throbs from me.

Adam. Call it straightway back.
Death's consummation crowns completed life,
Or comes too early. Hope being set on thee
For others; if for others, then for thee,—
For thee and me.

[*The wind revolves from the east, and round again to the east, perfumed by the Eden flower, and full of voices which sweep out into articulation as they pass.*

Let thy soul shake its leaves,
To feel the mystic wind—Hark!

Eve. I hear life.

Infant voices passing in the wind.

O we live, O we live—
And this life that we receive,
Is a warm thing and a new,
Which we softly bud into,
From the heart and from the brain,—
Something strange, that overmuch is
Of the sound and of the sight,
Flowing round in trickling touches,
In a sorrow and delight,—
Yet is it all in vain?
Rock us softly,
Lest it be all in vain.

Youthful voices passing.

O we live, O we live—

And this life that we achieve,
Is a loud thing and a bold,
Which, with pulses manifold,
Strikes the heart out full and fain—
Active doer, noble liver,
  Strong to struggle, sure to conquer,—
Though the vessel's prow will quiver
  At the lifting of the anchor:
Yet do we strive in vain?

Infant voices passing.

Rock us softly,
Lest it be all in vain.

Poet voices passing.

O we live, O we live—
And this life that we conceive,
Is a clear thing and a fair,
Which we set in crystal air,
That its beauty may be plain:
With a breathing and a flooding
  Of the heaven-life on the whole,
While we hear the forests budding
  To the music of the soul—
Yet is it tuned in vain?

Infant voices passing.

Rock us softly,
Lest it be all in vain.

Philosophic voices passing.

O we live, O we live—
And this life that we perceive,
Is a strong thing and a grave,
Which for others' use we have,

Duty-laden to remain.
We are helpers, fellow-creatures,
  Of the right against the wrong,—
We are earnest-hearted teachers
  Of the truth which maketh strong—
Yet do we teach in vain?

Infant voices passing.

Rock us softly,
Lest it be all in vain.

Revel voices passing.

O we live, O we live—
And this life that we reprieve,
Is a low thing and a light,
Which is jested out of sight,
And made worthy of disdain!
Strike with bold electric laughter
  The high tops of things divine—
Turn thy head, my brother, after,
  Lest thy tears fall in my wine;—
For is all laughed in vain?

Infant voices passing.

Rock us softly,
Lest it be all in vain.

Eve. I hear a sound of life—of life like ours—
Of laughter and of wailing,—of grave speech,
Of little plaintive voices innocent,—
Of life in separate courses flowing out
Like our four rivers to some outward main.
I hear life—life!

Adam. And, so, thy cheeks have snatched
Scarlet to paleness; and thine eyes drink fast

Of glory from full cups; and thy moist lips
Seem trembling, both of them, with earnest doubts
Whether to utter words, or only smile.

Eve. Shall I be mother of the coming life?
Hear the steep generations, how they fall
Adown the visionary stairs of Time,
Like supernatural thunders—far, yet near;
Sowing their fiery echoes through the hills.
Am I a cloud to these—mother to these?

Earth Spirits. And bringer of the curse upon all
these.

EVE *sinks down again.*

Poet voices passing.

O we live, O we live—
And this life that we believe,
Is a noble thing and high,
Which we climb up loftily,
To view God without a stain:
Till recoiling where the shade is,
We retread our steps again,
And descend the gloomy Hades,
To resume man's mortal pain.
Shall it be climbed in vain?

Infant voices passing.

Rock us softly,
Lest it be all in vain.

Love voices passing.

O we live, O we live—
And this life we would retrieve,
Is a faithful thing apart,
Which we love in, heart to heart,

Until one heart fitteth twain.
"Wilt thou be one with me?"
"I will be one with thee!"
"Ha, ha!—we love and live!"
Alas! ye love and die!
Shriek—who shall reply?
For is it not loved in vain?

Infant voices passing.

Rock us softly,
Though it be all in vain.

Aged voices passing.

O we live, O we live—
And this life that we receive,
Is a gloomy thing and brief,
Which consummated in grief,
Leaving ashes for all gain.
Is it not *all* in vain?

Infant voices passing.

Rock us softly,
Though it be *all* in vain.

Voices die away.

Earth Spirits. And bringer of the curse upon all these.

Eve. The voices of foreshown Humanity
Die off;—so let me die.

Adam. So let us die,
When God's will soundeth the right hour of death.

Earth Spirits. And bringer of the curse upon all these.

Eve. O spirits! by the gentleness ye use
In winds at night, and floating clouds at noon,—

In gliding waters under lily leaves,—
In chirp of crickets, and the settling hush
A bird makes in her nest, with feet and wings,—
Fulfil your natures now!

Earth Spirits.

Agreed; allowed!
We gather out our natures like a cloud,
And thus fulfil their lightnings! Thus, and thus!
Hearken, O hearken to us!

First Spirit.

As the east wind blows bleakly in the norland,—
As the snow wind beats blindly from the moorland,—
As the simoon drives wild across the desert,—
As the thunder roars deep in the Unmeasured,—
As the torrent tears an ocean-world to atoms,—
As the whirlpool grinds fathoms below fathoms,—
Thus,—and thus!

Second Spirit.

As the yellow toad, that spits its poison chilly,—
As the tiger, in the jungle, crouching stilly,—
As the wild boar, with ragged tusks of anger,—
As the wolf-dog, with teeth of glittering clangour,—
As the vultures that scream against the thunder,—
As the owlets that sit and moan asunder,—
Thus,—and thus!

Eve. Adam! God!

Adam. Ye cruel, cruel, unrelenting Spirits!
By the power in me of the sovran soul,
Whose thoughts keep pace yet with the angel's march,
I charge you into silence—trample you

Down to obedience.—I am king of you!

Earth Spirits.

Ha, ha! thou art king!
With a sin for a crown,
And a soul undone:
Thou, who antagonized,
Tortured and agonized,
Art held in the ring
Of the zodiac!
Now, king, beware!
We are many and strong,
Whom thou standest among,—
And we press on the air,
And we stifle thee back,
And we multiply where
Thou wouldst trample us down
From rights of our own
To an utter wrong—
And, from under the feet of thy scorn,
O forlorn!
We shall spring up like corn,
And our stubble be strong.

Adam. God, there is power in Thee! I make appeal
Unto thy kingship.

Eve. There is pity in THEE,
O sinned against, great God!—My seed, my seed,
There is hope set on THEE—I cry to thee,
Thou mystic seed that shalt be!—leave us not
In agony beyond what we can bear,
Fallen in debasement below thunder-mark

A mark for scorning—taunted and perplext
By all these creatures we ruled yesterday,
Whom thou, Lord, rulest alway. O my Seed,
Through the tempestuous years that rain so thick
Betwixt my ghostly vision and thy face,
Let me have token! for my soul is bruised
Before the serpent's head.

[*A vision of* CHRIST *appears in the midst of the zodiac, which pales before the heavenly light. The Earth Spirits grow grayer and fainter.*

CHRIST. Lo, I AM HERE!

Adam. This is God!—Curse us not, God, any more.

Eve. But gazing so—so—with omnific eyes,
Lift my soul upward till it touch thy feet!
Or lift it only,—not to seem too proud,—
To the low height of some good angel's feet—
For such to tread on, when he walketh straight,
And thy lips praise him.

CHRIST. Spirits of the earth,
I meet you with rebuke for the reproach
And cruel and unmitigated blame
Ye cast upon your masters. True, they have sinned;
And true their sin is reckoned into loss
For you the sinless. Yet, your innocence,
Which of you praises? since God made your acts
Inherent in your lives, and bound your hands
With instincts and imperious sanctities,
From self-defacement? Which of you disdains
These sinners, who, in falling, proved their height
Above you, by their liberty to fall?
And which of you complains of loss by them,

For whose delight and use ye have your life
And honor in creation? Ponder it!
This regent and sublime Humanity,
Though fallen, exceeds you! this shall film your sun,—
Shall hunt your lightning to its lair of cloud,—
Turn back your rivers, footpath all your seas,
Lay flat your forests, master with a look
Your lion at his fasting, and fetch down
Your eagle flying. Nay, without this rule
Of mandom, ye would perish,—beast by beast
Devouring; tree by tree, with strangling roots
And trunks set tuskwise. Ye would gaze on God
With imperceptive blankness up the stars,
And mutter, "Why, God, hast thou made us thus?"
And, pining to a sallow idiocy,
Stagger up blindly against the ends of life;
Then stagnate into rottenness, and drop
Heavily—poor, dead matter—piecemeal down
The abysmal spaces—like a little stone
Let fall to chaos. Therefore, over you,
Accept this sceptre; therefore be content
To minister with voluntary grace
And melancholy pardon, every rite
And service in you, to this sceptred hand.
Be ye to man as angels be to God,
Servants in pleasure, singers of delight,
Suggesters to his soul of higher things
Than any of your highest. So, at last,
He shall look round on you, with lids too straight
To hold the grateful tears, and thank you well;
And bless you when he prays his secret prayers,

And praise you when he sings his open songs,
For the clear song-note he has learnt in you,
Of purifying sweetness ; and extend
Across your head his golden fantasies,
Which glorify you into soul from sense !
Go serve him for such price. That not in vain ;
Nor yet ignobly ye shall serve, I place
My word here for an oath, mine oath for act
To be hereafter. In the name of which
Perfect redemption and perpetual grace,
I bless you through the hope and through the peace,
Which are mine,—to the Love, which is myself.

Eve. Speak on still, Christ. Albeit thou bless me not
In set words, I am blessed in hearkening thee—
Speak, Christ.

CHRIST. Speak, Adam. Bless the woman, man—
It is thine office.

Adam. Mother of the world,
Take heart before this Presence. Lo ! my voice,
Which, naming erst the creatures, did express,—
God breathing through my breath,—the attributes
And instincts of each creature in its name ;
Floats to the same afflatus,—floats and heaves
Like a water-weed that opens to a wave,—
A full-leaved prophecy affecting thee,
Out fairly and wide. Henceforward, rise, aspire
Unto the calms and magnanimities,
The lofty uses, and the noble ends,
The sanctified devotion and full work,
To which thou art elect for evermore,

First woman, wife, and mother.
Eve. And first in sin.
Adam. And also the sole bearer of the Seed
Whereby sin dieth! Raise the majesties
Of thy disconsolate brows, O well-beloved,
And front with level eyelids the To come,
And all the dark o' the world. Rise, woman, rise
To thy peculiar and best altitudes
Of doing good and of enduring ill,—
Of comforting for ill, and teaching good,
And reconciling all that ill and good
Unto the patience of a constant hope,—
Rise with thy daughters! If sin came by thee,
And by sin, death,—the ransom-righteousness,
The heavenly life and compensative rest
Shall come by means of thee. If wo by thee
Had issue to the world, thou shalt go forth
An angel of the wo thou didst achieve;
Found acceptable to the world instead
Of others of that name, of whose bright steps
Thy deed stripped bare the hills. Be satisfied;
Something thou hast to bear through womanhood—
Peculiar suffering answering to the sin;
Some pang paid down for each new human life;
Some weariness in guarding such a life—
Some coldness from the guarded; some mistrust
From those thou hast too well served; from those beloved
Too loyally, some treason: feebleness
Within thy heart, and cruelty without;
And pressures of an alien tyranny,

With its dynastic reasons of larger bones
And stronger sinews. But, go to! thy love
Shall chant itself its own beatitudes,
After its own life-working. A child's kiss,
Set on thy sighing lips, shall make thee glad:
A poor man, served by thee, shall make thee rich;
A sick man, helped by thee, shall make thee strong;
Thou shalt be served thyself by every sense
Of service which thou renderest. Such a crown
I set upon thy head,—Christ witnessing
With looks of prompting love—to keep thee clear
Of all reproach against the sin foregone,
From all the generations which succeed.
Thy hand which plucked the apple, I clasp close;
Thy lips which spake wrong counsel, I kiss close,—
I bless thee in the name of Paradise,
And by the memory of Edenic joys
Forfeit and lost;—by that last cypress tree
Green at the gate, which thrilled as we came out;
And by the blessed nightingale, which threw
Its melancholy music after us;—
And by the flowers, whose spirits full of smells
Did follow softly, plucking us behind
Back to the gradual banks and vernal bowers
And fourfold river-courses:—by all these,
I bless thee to the contraries of these;
I bless thee to the desert and the thorns,
To the elemental change and turbulence,
And to the roar of the estranged beasts,
And to the solemn dignities of grief,—
To each one of these ends,—and to this END

Of Death and the hereafter!
Eve. I accept
For me and for my daughters this high part,
Which lowly shall be counted. Noble work
Shall hold me in the place of garden-rest;
And in the place of Eden's lost delight,
Worthy endurance of permitted pain;
While on my longest patience there shall wait
Death's speechless angel, smiling in the east
Whence cometh the cold wind. I bow myself
Humbly henceforward on the ill I did,
That humbleness may keep it in the shade.
Shall it be so? Shall *I* smile, saying so?
O seed! O king! O God, who *shalt* be seed,—
What shall I say? As Eden's fountains swelled
Brightly betwixt their banks, so swells my soul
Betwixt Thy love and power!
And, sweetest thoughts
Of foregone Eden! now, for the first time
Since God said "Adam," walking through the trees,
I dare to pluck you, as I plucked erewhile
The lily or pink, the rose or heliotrope,
So pluck I you—so largely—with both hands,—
And throw you forward on the outer earth
Wherein we are cast out, to sweeten it.
Adam. As thou, Christ, to illume it, holdest Heaven
Broadly above our heads.
[*The* CHRIST *is gradually transfigured during the following phrases of dialogue, into humanity and suffering.*
Eve. O Saviour Christ,
Thou standest mute in glory, like the sun.

Adam. We worship in Thy silence, Saviour Christ.
Eve. Thy brows grow grander with a forecast wo,—
Diviner, with the possible of Death!
We worship in thy sorrow, Saviour Christ.
Adam. How do thy clear, still eyes transpierce our souls,
As gazing *through* them toward the Father-throne,
In a pathetical, full Deity,
Serenely as the stars gaze through the air
Straight on each other.
Eve. O pathetic Christ,
Thou standest mute in glory, like the moon.
CHRIST. Eternity stands alway fronting God;
A stern colossal image, with blind eyes,
And grand dim lips, that murmur evermore
God, God, God! While the rush of life and death,
The roar of act and thought, of evil and good,—
The avalanches of the ruining worlds
Tolling down space,—the new world's genesis
Budding in fire,—the gradual humming growth
Of the ancient atoms, and first forms of earth,
The slow procession of the swathing seas
And firmamental waters,—and the noise
Of the broad, fluent strata of pure airs,—
All these flow onward in the intervals
Of that reiterant, solemn sound of—GOD!
Which WORD, innumerous angels straightway lift
High on celestial altitudes of song
And choral adoration, and then drop
The burden softly; shutting the last notes
Hushed up in silver wings! I' the noon of time,

Nathless, that mystic-lipped Eternity
Shall wax as silent-dumb as Death himself,
While a new voice beneath the spheres shall cry,
"God! Why hast thou forsaken me, my God?"
And not a voice in Heaven shall answer it.

The transfiguration is complete in sadness.

Adam. Thy speech is of the Heavenlies; yet, O Christ,
Awfully human are thy voice and face!

Eve. My nature overcomes me from thine eyes.

CHRIST. Then in the noon of time, shall one from Heaven,
An angel fresh from looking upon God,
Descend before a woman, blessing her,
With perfect benediction of pure love,
For all the world in all its elements;
For all the creatures of earth, air, and sea;
For all men in the body and in the soul,
Unto all ends of glory and sanctity.

Eve. O pale, pathetic Christ—I worship thee!
I thank thee for that woman!

CHRIST. For, at last,
I, wrapping round me your humanity,
Which, being sustained, shall neither break nor burn
Beneath the fire of Godhead, will tread earth,
And ransom you and it, and set strong peace
Betwixt you and its creatures. With my pangs
I will confront your sins: and since your sins
Have sunken to all nature's heart from yours,
The tears of my clean soul shall follow them,
And set a holy passion to work clear

Absolute consecration. In my brow
Of kingly whiteness, shall be crowned anew
Your discrowned human nature. Look on me!
As I shall be uplifted on a cross
In darkness of eclipse and anguish dread,
So shall I lift up in my pierced hands,
Not into dark, but light—not unto death,
But life,—beyond the reach of guilt and grief,
The whole creation. Henceforth in my name
Take courage, O thou woman,—man, take hope!
Your graves shall be as smooth as Eden's sward,
Beneath the steps of your prospective thoughts;
And one step past them, a new Eden-gate
Shall open on a hinge of harmony,
And let you through to mercy. Ye shall fall
No more, within that Eden, nor pass out
Any more from it. In which hope, move on,
First sinners and first mourners. Live and love,—
Doing both nobly, because lowlily;
Live and work, strongly,—because patiently!
And for the deed of death, trust it to God,
That it be well done, unrepented of.
And not to loss. And thence with constant prayers
Fasten your souls so high, that constantly
The smile of your heroic cheer may float
Above all floods of earthly agonies,
Purification being the joy of pain!

[*The vision of* CHRIST *vanishes.* ADAM *and* EVE *stand in an ecstasy. The earth-zodiac pales away shade by shade, as the stars, star by star, shine out in the sky; and the following chant from the two Earth Spirits (as they sweep back into the zodiac and disappear with it) accompanies the process of change.*

Earth Spirits.

By the mighty work thus spoken
Both for living and for dying,
We, our homage-oath once broken,
Fasten back again in sighing;
And the creatures and the elements renew their covenanting.
Here, forgive us all our scorning;
Here, we promise milder duty;
And the evening and the morning
Shall re-organize in beauty,
A sabbath day in sabbath joy, for universal chanting.

And if, still, this melancholy
May be strong to overcome us;
If this mortal and unholy,
We still fail to cast out from us,—
And we turn upon you, unaware, your own dark influences;
If ye tremble when surrounded
By our forest pine and palm trees;
If we cannot cure the wounded
With our marjoram and balm trees;
And if your souls, all mournfully, sit down among your senses,—
Yet, O mortals, do not fear us,—
We are gentle in our languor;
And more good ye shall have near us,
Than any pain or anger;
And our God's refracted blessing, in our blessing, shall be given!

By the desert's endless vigil,
  We will solemnize your passions;
By the wheel of the black eagle
  We will teach you exaltations,
When he sails against the wind, to the white spot up
    in Heaven.

Ye shall find us tender nurses
  To your weariness of nature;
And our hands shall stroke the curse's
  Dreary furrows from the creature,
Till your bodies shall lie smooth in death, and straight
    and slumberful:
Then, a couch we will provide you,
  Where no summer heat shall dazzle;
Strewing on you and beside you
  Thyme and rosemary and basil—
And the cypress shall grow overhead, to keep all safe
    and cool.

Till the Holy blood awaited
  Shall be chrism around us running,
Whereby, newly-consecrated,
  We shall leap up in God's sunning,
To join the spheric company, where the pure worlds
    assemble;
While, renewed by new evangels,
  Soul-consummated, made glorious,
Ye shall brighten past the angels—
  Ye shall kneel to Christ victorious;

And the rays around His feet, beneath your sobbing
lips, shall tremble.

[*The phantastic vision has all passed; the earth-zodiac has broken like a belt, and dissolved from the desert. The Earth Spirits vanish; and the stars shine out above, bright and mild.*

CHORUS OF INVISIBLE ANGELS.

While ADAM *and* EVE *advance into the desert, hand in hand.*

Hear our heavenly promise,
Through your mortal passion!
Love ye shall have from us,
In a pure relation!
As a fish or bird
Swims or flies, if moving,
We, unseen, are heard
To live on by loving.
Far above the glances
Of your eager eyes,
Listen! we are loving!
Listen, through man's ignorances—
Listen, through God's mysteries—
Listen down the heart of things,
Ye shall hear our mystic wings
Murmurous with loving!
Through the opal door,
Listen evermore
How we live by loving!

First semichorus.

When your bodies, therefore,
Lie in grave or goal,
Softly will we care for

Every enfranchised soul!
Softly and unlothly,
Through the door of opal,
We will draw you soothly
Toward the Heavenly people.
Floated on a minor fine
Into the full chant divine,
We will draw you smoothly,—
While the human in the minor
Makes the harmony diviner:
Listen to our loving!

Second semichorus.

Then a sough of glory
Shall your entrance greet;
Ruffling round the doorway,
All the radiance it shall meet.
From the Heavenly throned centre
Heavenly voices shall repeat—
"Souls redeemed and pardoned, enter;
For the chrism on you is sweet."
And every angel in the place
Lowlily shall bow his face,
Folded fair on softened sounds,
Because upon your hands and feet
He images his Master's wounds:
Listen to our loving!

First semichorus.

So, in the universe's
Consummated undoing,
Our angels of white mercies
Shall hover round the ruin!

Their wings shall stream upon the flame,
As if incorporate of the same,
In elemental fusion;
And calm their faces shall burn out
With a pale and mastering thought,
And a steadfast looking of desire,
From out between the clefts of fire,—
While they cry, in the Holy's name.
To the final Restitution!
Listen to our loving!

Second semichorus.

So, when the day of God is
To the thick graves accompted;
Awaking the dead bodies,
The angel of the trumpet
Shall split the charnal earth
To the roots of the grave,
Which never before were slackened;
And quicken the charnal birth,
With his blast so clear and brave;
Till the Dead shall start and stand erect,
And every face of the burial-place
The awful, single look, reflect,
Wherewith he them awakened.
Listen to our loving!

***First** semichorus.*

But wild is the horse of Death!
He will leap up wild at the clamor
Above and beneath;
And where is his Tamer
On that last day,

When he crieth, Ha, ha!
To the trumpet's blare,
And paweth the earth's Aceldama?
When he tosseth his head,
The drear-white steed,
And ghastily champeth the last moon-ray,—
What angel there
Can lead him away,
That the living may rule for the Dead?

Second semichorus.

Yet a TAMER shall be found!
One more bright than seraph crowned,
And more strong than cherub bold;
Elder, too, than angel old,
By his gray eternities,—
He shall master and surprise
The steed of Death,
For He is strong, and He is fain;
He shall quell him with a breath,
And shall lead him where He will,
With a whisper in the ear,
Which it alone can hear—
Full of fear—
And a hand upon the mane,
Grand and still.

First semichorus.

Through the flats of Hades, where the souls assemble,
HE will guide the Death-steed, calm between their ranks;
While, like beaten dogs, they a little moan and tremble

To see the darkness curdle from the horse's glittering
flanks.
Through the flats of Hades where the dreary shade
is,—
Up the steep of Heaven, will the Tamer guide the
steed,—
Up the spheric circles—circle above circle,
We, who count the ages, shall count the tolling tread—
Every hoof-fall striking a blinder, blanker sparkle
From the stony orbs, which shall show as they were
dead.

Second semichorus.

All the way the Death-steed, with tolling hoofs, shall
travel,
Ashen gray the planets shall be motionless as stones;
Loosely shall the systems eject their parts coeval,—
Stagnant in the spaces shall float the pallid moons;
Suns that touch their apogees, reeling from their
level,
Shall run back on their axles, in wild, low, broken
tunes.

Chorus.

Up against the arches of the crystal ceiling,
Shall the horse's nostrils steam the blurting breath;
Up between the angels pale with silent feeling,
Will the Tamer, calmly, lead the horse of death.

Semichorus.

Cleaving all that silence, cleaving all that glory,
Will the Tamer lead him straightway to the Throne.
"Look out, O Jehovah, to this I bring before Thee,
With a hand nail-pierced,—I, who am thy Son."

Then the Eye Divinest, from the Deepest, flaming,
On the mystic courser, shall look out in fire:
Blind the beast shall stagger, where It overcame
him,—
Meek as lamb at pasture—bloodless in desire—
Down the beast shall shiver,—slain amid the taming,—
And, by Life essential, the phantasm Death expire.

A Voice. Gabriel, thou Gabriel!

Another Voice. What wouldst *thou* with me?

First Voice. I heard thy voice sound in the angels'
song;
And I would give thee question.

Second Voice. Question me.

First Voice. Why have I called thrice to my
Morning-star
And had no answer? All the stars are out,
And round the earth, upon their silver lives,
Wheel out the music of the inner life,
And answer in their places. Only in vain
I cast my voice against the outer rays
Of *my* star, shut in light behind the sun!
No more reply than from a breaking string,
Breaking when touched. Or is she *not* my star?
Where *is* my star—my star? Have ye cast down
Her glory like my glory? Has she waxed
Mortal, like Adam? Has she learnt to hate
Like any angel?

Second Voice. She is sad for thee:
All things grow sadder to thee, one by one.

Chorus. Live, work on, O Earthy!
By the Actual's tension,

Speed the arrow worthy
Of a pure ascension.
From the low earth round you,
Reach the heights above you;
From the stripes that wound you,
Seek the loves that love you!
God's divinest burneth plain
Through the crystal diaphane
Of our loves that love you.

First Voice. Gabriel, O Gabriel!

Second Voice. What wouldst *thou* with me?

First Voice. Is it true, O thou Gabriel, that the crown
Of sorrow which I claimed, another claims?
That HE claims THAT too?

Second Voice. Lost one, it is true.

First Voice. That HE will be an exile from His Heaven,
To lead those exiles homeward?

Second Voice. It is true.

First Voice. That HE will be an exile by His will,
As I by mine election!

Second Voice. It is true.

First Voice. That *I* shall stand sole exile finally,—
Made desolate for fruition?

Second Voice. It is true.

First Voice. Gabriel!

Second Voice. I hearken.

First Voice. Is it true besides—
Aright true—that mine orient star will give
Her name of 'Bright and Morning-Star' to HIM,—

And take the fairness of His virtue back,
To cover loss and sadness?

Second Voice. It is true.

First Voice. UNTRUE, UNTRUE! O Morning-star! O MINE!
Who sittest secret in a veil of light,
Far up the starry spaces, say,—*Untrue!*
Speak but so loud as doth a wasted moon
To Tyrrhene waters! I am Lucifer—

[*A pause. Silence in the stars.*

All things grow sadder to me, one by one.

Angel-chorus.

Exiled Human creatures,
Let your hope grow larger!
Larger grows the vision
Of the new delight.
From this chain of Nature's,
God is the Discharger;
And the Actual's prison
Opens to your sight.

Semichorus.

Calm the stars and golden,
In a light exceeding:
What their rays have measured,
Let your hearts fulfil!
These are stars beholden
By your eyes in Eden;
Yet, across the desert,
See them shining still.

Chorus. Future joy and far light

Working such relations,—
Hear us singing gently—
Exiled is not lost!
God, above the starlight,
God, above the patience,
Shall at last present ye
Guerdons worth the cost.
Patiently enduring,
Painfully surrounded,
Listen how we love you—
Hope the uttermost—
Waiting for that curing
Which exalts the wounded,
Hear us sing above you—
EXILED, BUT NOT LOST:

[*The stars shine on brightly, while* ADAM *and* EVE *pursue their way into the far wilderness. There is a sound through the silence, as of the falling tears of an angel.*

THE ROMAUNT OF THE PAGE.

A KNIGHT of gallant deeds,
  And a young page at his side
From the holy war in Palestine,
  Did slow and thoughtful ride,
As each were a palmer, and told for beads
  The dews of the eventide.

"O young page," said the knight,
  "A noble page art thou!
Thou fearest not to steep in blood
  The curls upon thy brow;
And once in the tent, and twice in the fight,
  Didst ward me a mortal blow—"

"O brave knight," said the page,
  "Or ere we hither came,
We talked in tent, we talked in field
  Of the bloody battle-game:
But here, below this greenwood bough,
  I cannot speak the same.

"Our troop is far behind,
The woodland calm is new;
Our steeds, with slow grass-muffled hoofs,
Tread deep the shadows through.
And in my mind, some blessing kind
Is dropping with the dew.

"The woodland calm is pure—
I cannot choose but have
A thought, from these, o' the beechen-trees
Which, in our England, wave;
And of the little finches fine,
Which sang there, while in Palestine
The warrior-hilt we drave.

"Methinks, a moment gone,
I heard my mother pray!
I heard, sir knight, the prayer for *me*
Wherein she passed away;
And I know the Heavens are leaning down
To hear what I shall say."

The page spake calm and high
As of no mean degree;
Perhaps he felt in nature's broad
Full heart, his own was free:
And the knight looked up to his lifted eye,
Then answered smilingly:—

"Sir Page, I pray your grace!
Certes, I meant not so

To cross your pastoral mood, sir page,
With the crook of the battle-bow;
But a knight may speak of a lady's face,
I trow, in any mood or place,
If the grasses die or grow.

"And this, I meant to say,—
My lady's face shall shine
As ladies' faces use, to greet
My Page from Palestine:
Or, speak she fair, or prank she gay,
She is no lady of mine.

"And this, I meant to fear,—
Her bower may suit thee ill!
For, sooth, in that same field and tent,
Thy *talk* was somewhat still;
And fitter thy hand for my knightly spear,
Than thy tongue for my lady's will."

Slowly and thankfully
The young page bowed his head:
His large eyes seemed to muse a smile,
Until he blushed instead;
And no lady in her bower pardiè,
Could blush more sudden red—
"Sir Knight,—thy lady's bower to me,
Is suited well," he said.

Beati, beati, mortui!
From the convent on the sea,—

One mile off, or scarce as nigh,
Swells the dirge as clear and high
As if, that, over brake and lea,
Bodily the wind did carry
The great altar of St. Mary,
And the fifty tapers burning o'er it,
And the lady Abbess dead before it,—
And the chanting nuns whom yesterweek
Her voice did charge and bless—
Chanting steady, chanting meek,
Chanting with a solemn breath
Because that they are thinking less
Upon the Dead than upon death!
Beati, beati, mortui!
Now the vision in the sound
Wheeleth on the wind around—
Now it sweeps aback, away—
The uplands will not let it stay
To dark the western sun.
Mortui!—away at last,—
Or ere the page's blush is past!
And the knight heard all, and the page heard none.

"A boon, thou noble knight,
If ever I served thee!
Though thou art a knight, and I am a page,
Now grant a boon to me—
And tell me sooth, if dark or bright,
If little loved, or loved aright,
Be the face of thy ladye."

Gloomily looked the knight;
  "As a son thou hast served me:
And would to none, I had granted boon,
  Except to only thee!
For haply then I should love aright,—
For then I should know if dark or bright
  Were the face of my ladye.

"Yet ill it suits my knightly tongue
  To grudge that granted boon:
That heavy price, from heart and life
  I paid in silence down:
The hand that claimed it, cleared in fine
My father's fame: I swear by mine,
  That price was nobly won.

"Earl Walter was a brave old earl,—
  He was my father's friend;
And while I rode the lists at court,
  And little guessed the end,—
My noble father in his shroud,
Against a slanderer lying loud,
  He rose up to defend.

"Oh, calm, below the marble gray
  My father's dust was strown!
Oh, meek, above the marble gray,
  His image prayed alone!
The slanderer lied—the wretch was brave,—
For, looking up the minster-nave,

He saw my father's knightly glaive
  Was changed from steel to stone.

"But Earl Walter's glaive was steel,
  With a brave old hand to wear it!
And dashed the lie back in the mouth
Which lied against the godly truth
  And against the knightly merit:
The slanderer, 'neath the avenger's heel,
Struck up the dagger in appeal
From stealthy lie to brutal force—
And out upon that traitor's corse,
  Was yielded the true spirit.

"I would my hand had fought that fight,
  And justified my father!
I would my heart had caught that wound,
  And slept beside him rather!
I think it were a better thing
Than murthered friend, and marriage-ring,
  Forced on my life together.

"Wail shook Earl Walter's house—
  His true wife shed no tear—
She lay upon her bed as mute
  As the earl did on his bier:
Till—'Ride, ride fast,' she said at last,
'And bring the avengèd's son anear!
Ride fast—ride free, as a dart can flee:
For white of ble, with waiting for me,
  Is the corse in the next chambère.'

"I came—I knelt beside her bed—
  Her calm was worse than strife—
'My husband, for thy father dear,
Gave freely, when thou wert not here,
  His own and eke my life.
A boon! Of that sweet child we make
An orphan for thy father's sake,
  Make thou, for ours, a wife.'

"I said, 'My steed neighs in the court:
  My bark rocks on the brine;
And the warrior's vow, I am under now,
  To free the pilgrim's shrine:
But fetch the ring, and fetch the priest,
  And call that daughter of thine;
And rule she wide, from my castle on Nyde,
  While I am in Palestine.'

"In the dark chambère, if the bride was fair,
  Ye wis, I could not see;
But the steed thrice neighed, and the priest fast
    prayed
  And wedded fast were we.
Her mother smiled upon her bed,
As at its side we knelt to wed;
And the bride rose from her knee,
And kissed the smile of her mother dead,
  Or ever she kissed me.

"My page, my page, what grieves thee so,
  That the tears run down thy face?"—

"Alas, alas! mine own sistèr
Was in thy lady's case!
But *she* laid down the silks she wore
And followed him she wed before,
Disguised as his true servitor,
To the very battle-place."

And wept the page, and laughed the knight,
A careless laugh laughed he:
"Well done it were for thy sistèr,
But not for my ladye!
My love, so please you, shall requite
No woman, whether dark or bright,
Unwomaned if she be."

The page stopped weeping, and smiled cold—
"Your wisdom may declare
That womanhood is proved the best
By golden brooch and glossy vest
The mincing ladies wear:
Yet is it proved, and was of old,
Anear as well—I dare to hold—
By truth, or by despair."

He smiled no more—he wept no more.—
But passionate he spake,—
"Oh, womanly, she prayed in tent,
When none beside did wake!
Oh, womanly, she paled in fight,
For one belovèd's sake!—
And her little hand defiled with blood,

Her tender tears of womanhood,
 Most woman-pure, did make!"

"Well done it were for thy sistèr—
 Thou tellest well her tale!
But for my lady, she shall pray
 I' the kirk of Nydesdale—
Not dread for me, but love for me,
 Shall make my lady pale:
No casque shall hide her woman's tear—
It shall have room to trickle clear
 Behind her woman's veil."

"But what if she mistook thy mind,
 And followed thee to strife;
Then kneeling, did entreat thy love,
 As Paynims ask for life?"
"I would forgive, and evermore
Would love her as my servitor,
 But little as my wife.

"Look up—there is a small bright cloud
 Alone amid the skies!
So high, so pure, and so apart,
 A woman's glory lies."
The page looked up—the cloud was sheen—
A sadder cloud did rush, I ween,
 Betwixt it and his eyes:

Then dimly dropped his eyes away
 From welken unto hill—

Ha! who rides there?—the page is 'ware,
 Though the cry at his heart is still!
And the page seeth all, and the knight seeth none
Though banner and spear do fleck the sun,
 And the Saracens ride at will.

He speaketh calm, he speaketh low,—
 "Ride fast, my master, ride,
Or ere within the broadening dark
 The narrow shadows hide!"
"Yea, fast, my page; I will do so;
 And keep thou at my side."

"Now nay, now nay, ride on thy way,
 Thy faithful page precede!
For I must loose on saddle-bow
My battle-casque, that galls, I trow,
 The shoulder of my steed;
And I must pray, as I did vow,
 For one in bitter need.

"Ere night I shall be near to thee,—
 Now ride, my master, ride!
Ere night, as parted spirits cleave
To mortals too beloved to leave,
 I shall be at thy side."
The knight smiled free at the fantasy,
 And adown the dell did ride.

Had the knight looked up to the page's face,
 No smile the word had won!

Had the knight looked up to the page's face,
  I ween he had never gone:
Had the knight looked back to the page's geste,
  I ween he had turned anon:
For dread was the wo in the face so young;
And wild was the silent geste that flung
Casque, sword to earth—as the boy down-sprung,
  And stood—alone, alone.

He clenched his hands, as if to hold
  His soul's great agony—
"Have I renounced my womanhood,
  For wifehood unto *thee?*
And is this the last, last look of thine,
  That ever I shall see?

"Yet God thee save, and mayst thou have
  A lady to thy mind;
More woman-proud, and half as true
  As one thou leav'st behind!
And God me take with Him to dwell—
For Him I cannot love too well,
  As I have loved my kind."

She looketh up, in earth's despair,
  The hopeful Heavens to seek:
That little cloud still floateth there,
  Whereof her Loved did speak.
How bright the little cloud appears!
Her eyelids fall upon the tears,—
  And the tears, down either cheek.

The tramp of hoof, the flash of steel—
  The Paynims round her coming!
The sound and sight have made her calm,—
  False page, but truthful woman!
She stands amid them all unmoved:
The heart, once broken by the loved,
  Is strong to meet the foeman.

"Ho, Christian page! art keeping sheep,
  From pouring wine cups, resting?"—
"I keep my master's noble name,
  For warring, not for feasting:
And if that here Sir Hubert were,
My master brave, my master dear,
  Ye would not stay to question."

"Where is thy master, scornful page,
  That we may slay or bind him?"—
"Now search the lea, and search the wood,
  And see if ye can find him!
Nathless, as hath been often tried,
Your Paynim heroes faster ride
  Before him than behind him."

"Give smoother answers, lying page,
  Or perish in the lying."—
"I trow that if the warrior brand
Beside my foot, were in my hand,
  'Twere better at replying."
They cursed her deep, they smote her low,

They cleft her golden ringlets through:
   The Loving is the Dying.

She felt the scimitar gleam down,
   And met it from beneath,
With smile more bright in victory
   Than any sword from sheath,—
Which flashed across her lip serene,
Most like the spirit-light between
   The darks of life and death.

   Ingemisco, ingemisco!
From the convent on the sea,
Now it sweepeth solemnly!
As over wood and over lea,
Bodily the wind did carry
The great altar of St. Mary,
And the fifty tapers paling o'er it,
And the Lady Abbess stark before it,
And the weary nuns, with hearts that faintly
Beat along their voices saintly—
   Ingemisco, ingemisco!
Dirge for abbess laid in shroud,
Sweepeth o'er the shroudless Dead,
Page or lady, as we said,
With the dews upon her head,
All as sad if not as loud:
   Ingemisco, ingemisco!
Is ever a lament begun
By any mourner under sun,
Which, ere it endeth, suits but *one?*

THE LAY OF THE BROWN ROSARY.

PART FIRST

"ONORA, ONORA"—her mother is calling—
She sits at the lattice and hears the dew falling
Drop after drop from the sycamores laden
With dew as with blossom, and calls home the maiden—
"Night cometh, Onora."

She looks down the garden-walk caverned with trees,
To the limes at the end, where the green arbor is—
"Some sweet thought or other may keep were it found her,
While, forgot or unseen in the dreamlight around her—
Night cometh, Onora!"

She looks up the forest whose alleys shoot on
Like the mute minster-aisles, when the anthem is done,
And the choristers, sitting with faces aslant,
Feel the silence to consecrate more than the chant—
"Onora, Onora!"

And forward she looketh across the brown heath—
"Onora, art coming?"—What is it she seeth?
Nought, nought, but the gray border-stone that is wist
To dilate and assume a wild shape in the mist—
"My daughter!"—Then over

The casement she leaneth, and as she doth so,
She is 'ware of her little son playing below:
"Now where is Onora?"—He hung down his head
And spake not, then answering blushed scarlet-red,—
"At the tryst with her lover."

But his mother was wroth. In a sternness quoth she,
"As thou play'st at the ball, art thou playing with
me?
When we know that her lover to battle is gone,
And the saints know above that she loveth but one,
And will ne'er wed another?"

Then the boy wept aloud. 'Twas a fair sight, yet sad,
To see the tears run down the sweet blooms he had:
He stamped with his foot, said—"The saints know I
lied,
Because truth that is wicked, is fittest to hide!
Must I utter it, mother?"

In his vehement childhood he hurried within,
And knelt at her feet as in prayer against sin;
But a child at a prayer never sobbeth as he—
'Oh! she sits with the nun of the brown rosarie,
At nights in the ruin!

"The old convent ruin the ivy rots off,
Where the owl hoots by day, and the toad is sun-
proof;
Where no singing-birds build; and the trees gaunt
and gray,
As in stormy sea-coasts, appear blasted one way—
But is *this* the wind's doing?

"A nun in the east wall was buried alive,
Who mocked at the priest, when he called her to
shrive,—
And shrieked such a curse as the stone took her breath,
The old abbess fell backward and swooned unto death
With an ave half-spoken.

"I tried once to pass it, myself and my hound,
Till, as fearing the lash, down he shivered to ground!
A brave hound, my mother! a brave hound, ye wot!
And the wolf thought the same, with his fangs at her
throat,
In the pass of the Brocken.

"At dawn and at eve, mother, who sitteth there,
With the brown rosarie never used for a prayer?
Stoop low, mother, low! If we went there to see,
What an ugly great hole in that east wall must be
At dawn and at even!

"Who meet there, my mother, at dawn and at even?
Who meet by that wall, never looking to heaven?
O sweetest my sister, what doeth with *thee*,

The ghost of a nun with a brown rosarie,
And a face turned from heaven?

"St. Agnes o'erwatcheth my dreams; and erewhile
I have felt through mine eyelids, the warmth of her smile—
But last night, as a sadness like pity came o'er her,
She whispered—'Say *two* prayers at dawn for Onora!
The Tempted is sinning.'"

Onora, Onora! they heard her not coming—
Not a step on the grass, not a voice through the gloaming:
But her mother looked up, and she stood on the floor,
Fair and still as the moonlight that came there before,
And a smile just beginning:

It touches her lips—but it dares not arise
To the height of the mystical sphere of her eyes:
And the large musing eyes, neither joyous nor sorry,
Sing on like the angels in separate glory,
Between clouds of amber.

For the hair droops in clouds amber-colored, till stirred
Into gold by the gesture that comes with a word:
While—O soft!—her speaking is so interwound
Of the dim and the sweet, 'tis a twilight of sound,
And floats through the chamber.

"Since thou shrivest my brother, fair mother," said she,

"I count on thy priesthood for marrying of me:
And I know by the hills, that the battle is done—
That my lover rides on—will be here with the sun,
'Neath the eyes that behold thee!"

Her mother sat silent—too tender, I wis,
Of the smile her dead father smiled dying to kiss;
But the boy started up, pale with tears, passion-wrought,—
"O wicked fair sister, the hills utter nought!
If he cometh, who told thee?"

"I know by the hills," she resumed calm and clear,
"By the beauty upon them, that HE is anear:
Did they ever look *so* since he bade me adieu?
Oh, love in the waking, sweet brother, is true
As St. Agnes in sleeping."

Half-ashamed and half-softened, the boy did not speak,
And the blush met the lashes which fell on his cheek:
She bowed down to kiss him—Dear saints, did he see
Or feel on her bossom the BROWN ROSARIE—
That he shrank away weeping?

PART SECOND.

A bed—ONORA *sleeping.* Angels, *but not near.*

First Angel.

Must we stand so far, and she
So very fair?

Second Angel.

As bodies be.

First Angel.

And she so mild?

Second Angel.

As spirits, when
They meeken, not to God, but men.

First Angel.

And she so young,—that I who bring
Good dreams for saintly children, might
Mistake that small soft face to-night,
And fetch her such a blessed thing,
That, at her waking, she would weep
For childhood lost anew in sleep:
How hath she sinned?

Second Angel.

In bartering love—
God's love—for man's:

First Angel.

We may reprove
The world for this! not only her:—
Let me approach, to breathe away
This dust o' the heart with holy air.

Second Angel.

Stand off! She sleeps, and did not pray.

First Angel.

Did none pray for her?

Second Angel.

Ay, a child,—
Who never, praying, wept before:
While, in a mother undefiled,
Prayer goeth on in sleep, as true
And pauseless as the pulses do

First Angel.

Then I approach.

Second Angel.

It is not WILLED.

First Angel.

One word: Is she redeemed?

Second Angel.

No more!
THE PLACE IS FILLED. [Angels *vanish.*

Evil Spirit in a Nun's garb by the bed.

Forbear that dream—forbear that dream! too near to Heaven it leaned.

Onora in sleep.

Nay, leave me this—but only this! 'tis but a dream, sweet fiend!

Evil Spirit.

It is a *thought.*

Onora in sleep.

A sleeping thought—most innocent of good—
It doth the Devil no harm, sweet fiend! it cannot, if it would.
I say in it no holy hymn,—I do no holy work;

I scarcely hear the sabbath-bell that chimeth from the kirk.

Evil Spirit.

Forbear that dream—forbear that dream!

Onora in sleep.

Nay, let me *dream* at least:
That far-off bell, it may be took for viol at a feast—
I only walk among the fields, beneath the summer-sun,
With my dead father, hand in hand, as I have often done.

Evil Spirit.

Forbear that dream—forbear that dream!

Onora in sleep.

Nay, sweet fiend, let me go—
I never more can walk with *him*, O nevermore but so:
For they have tied my father's feet beneath the kirk-yard stone,—
Oh, deep and straight; oh, very straight! they move at nights alone:
And then he calleth through my dreams, he calleth tenderly,—
'Come forth, my daughter, my beloved, and walk the fields with me!'

Evil Spirit.

Forbear that dream, or else disprove its pureness by a sign.

Onora in sleep.

Speak on, thou shalt be satisfied! my word shall answer thine.
I hear a bird which used to sing when I a child was praying;

I see the poppies in the corn I used to sport away in.
What shall I do—tread down the dew, and pull the blossoms blowing?
Or clap my wicked hands to fright the finches from the rowen?

Evil Spirit.

Thou shalt do something harder still: Stand up where thou dost stand,
Among the fields of Dreamland, with thy father, hand in hand,
And clear and slow, repeat the vow—declare its cause and kind,
Which, not to break in sleep or wake, thou bearest on thy mind.

Onora in sleep.

I bear a vow of wicked kind, a vow for mournful cause:
I vowed it deep, I vowed it strong—the spirits laughed applause:
The spirits trailed, along the pines, low laughter like a breeze,
While, high atween their swinging tops, the stars appeared to freeze.

Evil Spirit.

More calm and free,—speak out to me, why such a vow was made.

Onora in sleep.

Because that God decreed my death, and I shrank back afraid:
Have patience, O dead father mine! I did not fear to die;-

I wish I were a young dead child, and had thy company!
I wish I lay beside thy feet, a buried three-year child,
And wearing only a kiss of thine, upon my lips that smiled!
The linden-tree that covers thee, might, so, have shadowed twain—
For death itself I did not fear—'tis love that makes the pain.
Love feareth death: I was no child—I was betrothed that day;
I wore a troth-kiss on my lips, I could not give away:
How could I bear to lie content and still beneath a stone,
And feel mine own Betrothed go by—alas! no more mine own,—
Go leading by, in wedding pomp, some lovely lady brave,
With cheeks that blushed as red as rose, while mine were cold in grave?
How could I bear to sit in Heaven, on e'er so high a throne,
And hear him say to her—to *her!* that else he loveth none?
Though e'er so high I sate above, though e'er so low he spake,
As clear as thunder I should hear the new oath he might take—
That *hers,* forsooth, are heavenly eyes,—ah, me! while very dim

Some heavenly eyes (indeed of Heaven!) would darken down to *him*.

Evil Spirit.

Who told thee thou wert called to death?

Onora in sleep.

I sat all night beside thee—
The gray owl on the ruined wall shut both his eyes to hide thee;
And ever he flapped his heavy wing, all brokenly and weak,
And the long grass waved against the sky, around his gasping beak:
I sat beside thee all the night, while the moonlight lay forlorn
Strewn round us like a dead world's shroud, in ghastly fragments torn:
And through the night, and through the hush, and over the flapping wing,
We heard, beside the Heavenly Gate, the angels murmuring:—
We heard them say, 'Put day to day, and count the days to seven,
'And God will draw Onora up the golden stairs of Heaven:
'And yet the evil ones have leave that purpose to defer,
'For if she has no need of HIM, He has no need of *her*'—

Evil Spirit.

Speak out to me—speak bold and free.

Onora in sleep.

And then I heard thee say,—
'I count upon my rosarie brown, the hours thou hast to stay!
'Yet God permits us evil ones to put by that decree,
'Since if thou hast no need of HIM, He has no need of *thee*—
'And if thou wilt forego the sight of angels, verily
'Thy true love gazing on thy face, shall guess what angels be—
'Nor bride shall pass, save thee' . . . Alas!—my father's hand's acold—
The meadows seem. . . .

Evil Spirit.

Forbear the dream, or let the vow be told!

Onora in sleep.

I vowed upon thy rosarie brown, this string of antique beads,
By charnal lichens overgrown, and dank among the weeds—
This rosarie brown which is thine own,—lost soul of buried nun,—
Who, lost by vow, wouldst render now all souls alike undone;—
I vowed upon thy rosarie brown,—and, till such vow should break,
A pledge always of living days, 'twas hung around my neck —
I vowed to thee on rosarie, (Dead father, look not so!)
I would not thank God in my weal, nor seek God in my wo.

Evil Spirit.

And canst thou prove . . . .

Onora in sleep.

O love—my love! I felt him near again!
I saw his steed on mountain-head, I heard it on the plain!
Was this no weal for me to feel?—is greater weal than this?
Yet when he came, I wept his name—and the angels heard but *his.*

Evil Spirit.

Well done, well done!

Onora in sleep.

Ay me! the sun . . . the dreamlight 'gins to pine,—
Ay me! how dread can look the Dead!—Aroint thee, father mine!

She starteth from slumber, she sitteth upright,
And her breath comes in sobs while she stares through the night:
There is nought: The great willow, her lattice before,
Large-drawn in the moon, lieth calm on the floor;
But her hands tremble fast as their pulses, and free
From the death-clasp, close over—the BROWN ROSARIE.

THIRD PART.

'Tis a morn for a bridal; the merry bride-bell
Rings clear through the green-wood that skirts the
chapelle;
And the priest at the altar awaiteth the bride,
And the sacristans slyly are jesting aside
At the work shall be doing.

While down through the wood rides that fair company,
The youths with the courtship, the maids with the
glee,—
Till the chapel-cross opens to sight, and at once
All the maids sigh demurely, and think for the nonce,
'And so endeth a wooing!'

And the bride and the bridegroom are leading the
way,
With his hand on her rein, and a word yet to say:
Her dropt eyelids suggest the soft answers beneath,—
And the little quick smiles come and go with her
breath,
When she sigheth or speaketh.

And the tender bride-mother breaks off unaware
From an Ave, to think that her daughter is fair,—
Till in nearing the chapel, and glancing before,
She seeth her little son stand at the door,—
Is it play that he seeketh?

Is it play? when his eyes wander innocent-wild,
And sublimed with a sadness unfitting a child!
He trembles not, weeps not—the passion is done,
And calmly he kneels in their midst, with the sun
On his head like a glory.

"O fair-featured maids, ye are many!" he cried,—
"But, in fairness and vileness, who matcheth the bride?
O brave-hearted youths, ye are many! but whom,
For the courage and wo, can ye match with the groom,
As ye see them before ye?"

Out spake the bride's mother—"The vileness is thine,
If thou shame thine own sister, a bride at the shrine!"
Out spake the bride's lover—"The vileness be mine,
If he shame mine own wife at the hearth or the shrine,
And the charge be unprovèd.

"Bring the charge, prove the charge, brother! speak it aloud—
Let thy father and hers, hear it deep in his shroud!"
—"O father, thou seest—for dead eyes can see—
How she wears on her bosom *a brown rosarie*,
O my father belovèd!"

Then outlaughed the bridegroom, and outlaughed withal
Both maidens and youths, by the old chapel-wall—
"So she weareth no love-gift, kind brother," quoth he,

"She may wear, an she listeth, a brown rosarie,
Like a pure-hearted lady!"

Then swept through the chapel, the long bridal train:
Though he spake to the bride, she replied not again:
On, as one in a dream, pale and stately she went,
Where the altar-lights burn o'er the great sacrament,
Faint with daylight, but steady.

But her brother had passed in between them and her,
And calmly knelt down on the high-altar stair—
Of an infantine aspect so stern to the view,
That the priest could not smile on the child's eyes of blue,
As he would for another.

He knelt like a child marble-sculptured and white,
That seems kneeling to pray on the tomb of a knight,
With a look taken up to each iris of stone
From the greatness and death where he kneeleth, but none
From the face of a mother.

"In your chapel, O priest, ye have wedded and shriven
Fair wives for the hearth, and fair sinners for Heaven!
But this fairest my sister, ye think now to wed,
Bid her kneel where she standeth, and shrive her instead—
O shrive her and wed not!"

In tears, the bride's mother,—"Sir priest, unto thee
Would he lie, as he lied to this fair company!"

In wrath, the bride's lover,—"The lie shall be clear!
Speak it out, boy! the saints in their niches shall
hear—
Be the charge proved or said not!"

Then serene in his childhood he lifted his face,
And his voice sounded holy and fit for the place—
"Look down from your niches, ye still saints, and see
How she wears on her bosom *a brown rosarie!*
Is it used for the praying?"

The youths looked aside—to laugh there were a sin—
And the maidens' lips trembled with smiles shut
within:
Quoth the priest—"Thou art wild, pretty boy!
Blessed she,
Who prefers at her bridal a brown rosarie
To a worldly arraying!"

The bridegroom spake low and led onward the bride,
And before the high altar they stood side by side:
The rite-book is opened, the rite is begun—
They have knelt down together to rise up as one—
Who laughed by the altar?

The maidens looked forward, the youths looked
around,—
The bridegroom's eye flashed from his prayer at the
sound;
And each saw the bride, as if no bride she were,

Gazing cold at the priest, without gesture of prayer,
As he read from the psalter.

The priest never knew that she did so, but still
He felt a power on him, too strong for his will;
And whenever the Great Name was there to be read,
His voice sank to silence—THAT could not be said,
Or the air could not hold it.

"I have sinned," quoth he, "I have sinned, I wot"—
And the tears ran adown his old cheeks at the thought;
They dropped fast on the book; but he read on the same,—
And aye was the silence where should be the NAME,
As the choristers told it.

The rite-book is closed, and the rite being done,
They who knelt down together, arise up as one:
Fair riseth the bride—Oh, a fair bride is she,—
But, for all (think the maidens) that brown rosarie,
No saint at her praying!

What aileth the bridegroom? He glares blank and wide—
Then suddenly turning, he kisseth the bride—
His lip stung her with cold: she glanced upwardly mute:
"Mine own wife," he said, and fell stark at her foot
In the word he was saying.

They have lifted him up,—but his head sinks away,—
And his face showeth bleak in the sunshine, and gray.

Leave him now where he lieth—for oh, nevermore
Will he kneel at an altar or stand on a floor!
Let his bride gaze upon him!

Long and still was her gaze, while they chafed him there,
And breathed in the mouth whose last life had kissed her:
But when they stood up—only *they!* with a start
The shriek from her soul struck her pale lips apart—
She has lived, and forgone him!

And low on his body she droppeth adown—
"Didst call me thine own wife, beloved—thine own?
Then take thine own with thee! thy coldness is warm
To the world's cold without thee! Come, keep me from harm
In a calm of thy teaching!"

She looked in his face earnest long, as in sooth
There were hope of an answer,—and then kissed his mouth;
And with head on his bosom, wept, wept bitterly,—
"Now, O God, take pity—take pity on me!—
God, hear my beseeching!"

She was 'ware of a shadow that crossed where she lay;
She was 'ware of a presence that wither'd the day—
Wild she sprang to her feet,—"I surrender to *thee*
The broken vow's pledge,—the accursed rosarie,—
I am ready for dying!"

She dashed it in scorn to the marble-paved ground,
Where it fell mute as snow; and a weird music-sound
Crept up, like a chill, up the aisles long and dim,—
As the fiends tried to mock at the choristers' hymn,
And moaned in the trying.

FOURTH PART.

Onora looketh listlessly adown the garden walk:
"I am weary, O my mother, of thy tender talk!
I am weary of the trees a-waving to and fro—
Of the steadfast skies above, the running brooks below;—
All things are the same but I;—only I am dreary;
And, mother, of my dreariness, behold me very weary.

"Mother, brother, pull the flowers I planted in the spring,
And smiled to think I should smile more upon their gathering.
The bees will find out other flowers—oh, pull them, dearest mine,
And carry them and carry me before St. Agnes' shrine."
—Whereat they pulled the summer flowers she planted in the spring,
And her and them, all mournfully, to Agnes' shrine did bring.

She looked up to the pictured saint, and gently shook her head—
"The picture is too calm for *me*—too calm for *me*," she said:
"The little flowers we brought with us, before it we may lay,
For those are used to look at heaven,—but *I* must turn away—
Because no sinner under sun, can dare or bear to gaze
On God's or angel's holiness, except in Jesu's face."

She spoke with passion after pause—"And were it wisely done,
If we who cannot gaze above, should walk the earth alone?—
If we whose virtue is so weak, should have a will so strong,—
And stand blind on the rocks, to choose the right path from the wrong?
To choose perhaps a love-lit hearth, instead of love and Heaven,—
A single rose, for a rose-tree, which beareth seven times seven?
A rose that droppeth from the hand, that fadeth in the breast,
Until, in grieving for the worst, we learn what is the best!"
Then breaking into tears,—"Dear God," she cried, "and must we see
All blissful things depart from *us*, or ere we go to Thee?

We cannot guess thee in the wood, or hear thee in the wind?
Our cedars must fall round us, ere we see the light behind?
Ay, sooth, we feel too strong in weal, to need thee on that road;
But wo being come, the soul is dumb, that crieth not on 'God.'"

Her mother could not speak for tears; she ever muséd thus—
"*The bees will find out other flowers*,—but what is left for *us?*"
But her young brother stayed his sobs, and knelt beside her knee,
—"Thou sweetest sister in the world, hast never a word for me?"
She passed her hand across his face, she pressed it on his cheek,
So tenderly, so tenderly—she needed not to speak.

The wreath which lay on shrine that day, at vespers bloomed no more—
The woman fair who placed it there, had died an hour before!
Both perished mute, for lack of root, earth's nourishment to reach;—
O reader, breathe (the ballad saith) some sweetness out of each!

LADY GERALDINE'S COURTSHIP.

A ROMANCE OF THE AGE

A poet writes to his friend. Place—A room in Wycombe Hall.
Time—Late in the evening.

DEAR my friend and fellow-student, I would lean my spirit o'er you;
Down the purple of this chamber, tears should scarcely run at will:
I am humbled who was humble! Friend,—I bow my head before you!
You should lead me to my peasants!—but their faces are too still.

There's a lady—an earl's daughter; she is proud and she is noble;
And she treads the crimson carpet, and she breathes the perfumed air;
And a kingly blood sends glances up her princely eye to trouble,
And the shadow of a monarch's crown is softened in her hair.

She has halls and she has castles, and the resonant
steam-eagles
Follow far on the direction of her little dove-like
hand—
Trailing on a thunderous vapor underneath the
starry vigils,
So to mark upon the blasted heaven, the measure of
her land.

There are none of England's daughters, who can show
a prouder presence;
Upon princely suitors suing, she has looked in her
disdain:
She was sprung of English nobles, I was born of
English peasants;
What was *I* that I should love her—save for feeling
of the pain?
I was only a poor poet, made for singing at her case-
ment,
As the finches or the thrushes, while she thought of
other things.
Oh, she walked so high above me, she appeared to my
abasement,
In her lovely silken murmur, like an angel clad in
wings!

Many vassals bow before her, as her chariot sweeps
their door-ways;
She has blest their little children,—as a priest or
queen were she!

Far too tender or too cruel far, her smile upon the poor was,
For I thought it was the same smile, which she used to smile on me.

She has voters in the commons, she has lovers in the palace—
And of all the fair court-ladies, few have jewels half as fine:
Even the prince has named her beauty, 'twixt the red wine and the chalice:
Oh, and what was *I* to love her? my Beloved, my Geraldine!

Yet I could not choose but love her—I was born to poet uses—
To love all things set above me, all of good and all of fair:
Nymphs of mountain, not of valley, we are wont to call the Muses—
And in nympholeptic climbing, poets pass from mount to star.

And because I was a poet, and because the people praised me,
With their critical deductions for the modern writer's fault;
I could sit at rich men's tables,—though the courtesies that raised me,
Still suggested clear between us, the pale spectrum of the salt.

And they praised me in her presence :—" Will your
book appear this summer ?"
Then returning to each other—" Yes, our plans are
for the moors ;"
Then with whisper dropped behind me—" There he
is ! the latest comer !
Oh, she only likes his verses ! what is over, she
endures.

" Quite low born ! self-educated ! somewhat gifted
though by nature,—
And we make a point of asking him,—of being very
kind ;
You may speak, he does not hear you ; and besides,
he writes no satire,—
These new charmers who keep serpents, have the
antique sting resigned."

I grew scornfuller, grew colder, as I stood up there
among them,—
Till as frost intense will burn you, the cold scorning
scorched my brow ;
When a sudden silver speaking, gravely cadenced,
overrung them,
And a sudden silken stirring touched my inner nature
through.

I looked upward and beheld her ! With a calm and
regnant spirit,
Slowly round she swept her eyelids, and said clear
before them all—

"Have you such superfluous honor, sir, that, able to
to confer it,
You will come down, Mr. Bertram, as my guest to
Wycombe Hall?"

Here she paused,—she had been paler at the first
word of her speaking;
But because a silence followed it, blushed scarlet, as
for shame;
Then, as scorning her own feeling, resumed calmly—
"I am seeking
More distinction than these gentlemen think worthy
of my claim.

"Ne'ertheless, you see, I seek it—not because I am
a woman,"—
(Here her smile sprang like a fountain, and, so, over-
flowed her mouth)
"But because my woods in Sussex have some purple
shades at gloaming,
Which are worthy of a king in state, or poet in his
youth.

"I invite you, Mr. Bertram, to no scene for worldly
speeches—
Sir, I scarce should dare—but only where God asked
the thrushes first—
And if *you* will sing beside them, in the covert of my
beeches,
I will thank you for the woodlands, . . . for the human
world at worst."

Then, she smiled around right childly, then, she gazed around right queenly;
And I bowed—I could not answer! Alternated light and gloom—
While as one who quells the lions, with a steady eye serenely,
She, with level fronting eyelids, passed out stately from the room.

Oh, the blessed woods of Sussex, I can hear them still around me,
With their leafy tide of greenery still rippling up the wind!
Oh, the cursed woods of Sussex! where the hunter's arrow found me,
When a fair face and a tender voice had made me mad and blind!

In that ancient hall of Wycombe, thronged the numerous guests invited,
And the lovely London ladies trod the floors with gliding feet;
And their voices low with fashion, not with feeling, softly freighted
All the air about the windows, with elastic laughters sweet.

For at eve, the open windows, flung their light out on
the terrace,
Which the floating orbs of curtains, did with gradual
shadow sweep;
While the swans upon the river, fed at morning by the
heiress,
Trembled downward through their snowy wings, at
music in their sleep.

And there evermore was music, both of instrument and
singing;
Till the finches of the shrubberies, grew restless in
the dark;
But the cedars stood up motionless, each in a moon-
light ringing,
And the deer, half in the glimmer, strewed the hollows
of the park.

And though sometimes she would bind me with her
silver-corded speeches,
To commix my words and laughter with the converse
and the jest,—
Oft I sat apart, and gazing on the river, through the
beeches,
Heard, as pure the swans swam down it, her pure
voice o'erfloat the rest

In the morning, horn of huntsman, hoof of steed, and
laugh of rider,
Spread out cheery from the court-yard, till we lost
them in the hills;

While herself and other ladies, and her suitors left beside her,
Went a-wandering up the gardens, through the laurels and abeles.

Thus, her foot upon the new-mown grass—bareheaded —with the flowing
Of the virginal white vesture, gathered closely to her throat;
With the golden ringlets in her neck, just quickened by her going,
And appearing to breathe sun for air, and doubting if to float,—

With a branch of dewy maple, which her right hand held above her,
And which trembled a green shadow in betwixt her and the skies,—
As she turned her face in going, thus, she drew me on to love her,
And to worship the divineness of the smile hid in her eyes.

For her eyes alone smile constantly: her lips have serious sweetness,
And her front is calm—the dimple rarely ripples on her cheek:
But her deep blue eyes smile constantly,—as if they had by fitness
Won the secret of a happy dream, she does not care to speak.

Thus she drew me the first morning, out across into
the garden :
And I walked among her noble friends, and could not
keep behind ;
Spake she unto all and unto me—" Behold, I am the
warden,
Of the song birds in these lindens, which are cages to
their mind.

" But within this swarded circle, into which the
lime-walk brings us—
Whence the beeches rounded greenly, stand away in
reverent fear ;
I will let no music enter, saving what the fountain
sings us,
Which the lilies round the basin, may seem pure
enough to hear.

" The live air that waves the lilies, waves this slender
jet of water,
Like a holy thought sent feebly up from soul of fast-
ing saint !
Whereby lies a marble Silence, sleeping ! (Lough the
sculptor wrought her,)
So asleep, she is forgetting to say *Hush !*—a fancy
quaint !

" Mark how heavy white her eyelids ! not a dream
between them lingers !
And the left hand's index droppeth from the lips upon
the cheek :

And the right hand,—with the symbol rose held slack within the fingers,—
Has fallen backward in the basin—yet this Silence will not speak!

"That the essential meaning growing, may exceed the special symbol,
Is the thought, as I conceive it: it applies more high and low,—
Our true noblemen will often, through right nobleness, grow humble,
And assert an inward honor, by denying outward show."

"Nay, your Silence," said I, "truly holds her symbol rose but slackly,
Yet *she holds it*—or would scarcely be a Silence to our ken!
And your nobles wear their ermine on the outside, or walk blackly
In the presence of the social law, as most ignoble men.

"Let the poets dream such dreaming! Madam, in these British islands,
'Tis the substance that wanes ever, 'tis the symbol that exceeds;
Soon we shall have nought but symbol! and for statues like this Silence,
Shall accept the rose's marble—in another case, the weed's."

"Not so quickly!" she retorted,—"I confess where'er you go, you
Find for things, names—shows for actions, and pure gold for honor clear;
But when all is run to symbol in the Social, I will throw you
The world's book, which now reads drily, and sit down with Silence here."

Half in playfulness she spoke, I thought, and half in indignation;
Friends who listened laughed her words off while her lovers deemed her fair,—
A fair woman—flushed with feeling, in her noble-lighted station,
Near the statue's white reposing—and both bathed in sunny air!

With the trees round, not so distant, but you heard their vernal murmur,
And beheld in light and shadow, the leaves in and outward move;
And the little fountain leaping toward the sun-heart to be warmer,
And recoiling backward, trembling with the too much light above—

'Tis a picture for remembrance! and thus, morning after morning,
Did I follow as she drew me, by the spirit, to her feet—

Why, her greyhound followed also! dogs—we both
were dogs for scorning—
To be sent back when she pleased it, and her path
lay through the wheat.

And thus, morning after morning, spite of oath, and
spite of sorrow,
Did I follow at her drawing, while the week-days
passed along;
Just to feed the swans this noontide, or to see the
fawns to-morrow,
Or to teach the hill-side echo, some sweet Tuscan in
a song.

Ay, and sometimes on the hill-side, while we sat down
in the gowans,
With the forest green behind us, and its shadow cast
before;
And the river running under; and across it, from the
rowans,
A brown partridge whirring near us, till we felt the
air it bore—

There, obedient to her praying, did I read aloud the
poems
Made by Tuscan flutes, or instruments more various,
of our own;
Read the pastoral parts of Spenser—or the subtle
interflowings
Found in Petrarch's sonnets—here's the book—the
leaf is folded down!—

Or at times a modern volume,—Wordsworth's solemn-thoughted idyl,
Howitt's ballad-dew, or Tennyson's enchanted reverie,—
Or from Browning some "Pomegranate," which, if cut deep down the middle,
Shows a heart within blood-tinctured, of a veined humanity!—

Or, at times I read there, hoarsely, some new poem of my making—
Poets ever fail in reading their own verses to their worth,—
For the echo, in you, breaks upon the words which you are speaking,
And the chariot-wheels jar in the gate, through which you drive them forth.

After, when we were grown tired of books, the silence round us flinging
A slow arm of sweet compression, felt with beatings at the breast,—
She would break out, on a sudden, in a gush of woodland singing,
Like a child's emotion in a god—a naiad tired of rest.

Oh, to see or hear her singing! scarce I know which is divinest—
For her looks sing too—she modulates her gestures on the tune;

And her mouth stirs with the song, like song; and when the notes are finest,
'Tis the eyes that shoot out vocal light, and seem to swell them on.

Then we talked—oh, how we talked! (her voice, so cadenced in the talking,
Made another singing—of the soul! a music without bars—)
While the leafy sounds of woodlands, humming round where we were walking,
Brought interposition worthy-sweet,—as skies about the stars.

And she spake such good thoughts natural, as if she always thought them—
And had sympathies so rapid, open, free as bird on branch,
Just as ready to fly east as west, whichever way besought them,
In the birchen wood a chirrup, or a cock-crow in the grange.

In her utmost lightness there is truth—and often she speaks lightly;
And she has a grace in being gay, which even mournful souls approve;
For the root of some grave earnest thought is understruck so rightly,
As to justify the foliage and the waving flowers above.

And she talked on—*we* talked, rather! upon all things—substance—shadow—
Of the sheep that browsed the grasses—of the reapers in the corn—
Of the little children from the schools, seen winding through the meadow—
Of the poor rich world beyond them, still kept poorer by its scorn.

So of men, and so, of letters—books are men of higher stature,
And the only men that speak aloud for future times to hear;
So, of mankind in the abstract, which grows slowly into nature,
Yet will lift the cry of "progress," as it trod from sphere to sphere.

And her custom was to praise me, when I said,—"The Age culls simples,
With a broad clown's back turned broadly, to the glory of the stars—
We are gods by our own reck'ning,—and may well shut up the temples,
And wield on, amid the incense-steam, the thunder of our cars.

"For we throw out acclamations of self-thanking, self-admiring,
With, at every mile run faster,—'O the wondrous, wondrous age,'

Little thinking if we work our SOULS as nobly as our
iron,—
Or if angels will commend us, at the goal of pil-
grimage.

"Why, what *is* this patient entrance into nature's
deep resources,
But the child's most gradual learning to walk upright
without bane?—
When we drive out, from the cloud of steam, majes-
tical white horses,
Are we greater than the first men, who led black ones
by the mane?

"If we trod the deeps of ocean, if we struck the stars in
rising,
If we wrapped the globe intensely with one hot elec-
tric breath,
'Twere but power within our *tether*—no new spirit-
power conferring—
And in life we were not greater men, nor bolder men
in death."

She was patient with my talking; and I loved her—
loved her certes,
As I loved all Heavenly objects, with uplifted eyes
and hands!
As I loved pure inspirations—loved the graces, loved
the virtues,—
In a Love content with writing his own name, on
desert sands.

Or at least I thought so purely!—thought, no idiot Hope was raising
Any crown to crown Love's silence—silent Love that sat alone—
Out, alas! the stag is like me—he, that tries to go on grazing
With the great deep gun-wound in his neck, then reels with sudden moan.

It was thus I reeled! I told you that her hand had many suitors—
But she smiles them down imperially, as Venus did, the waves—
And with such a gracious coldness, that they cannot press their futures
On the present of her courtesy, which yieldingly enslaves.

And this morning, as I sat alone within the inner chamber
With the great saloon beyond it, lost in pleasant thought serene—
For I had been reading Camoëns—that poem you remember,
Which his lady's eyes are praised in, as the sweetest ever seen.

And the book lay open, and my thought flew from it, taking from it
A vibration and impulsion to an end beyond its own,—

As the branch of a green osier, when a child would overcome it,
Springs up freely from his clasping, and goes swinging in the sun.

As I mused I heard a murmur,—it grew deep as it grew longer—
Speakers using earnest language—"Lady Geraldine, you *would!*"
And I heard a voice that pleaded ever on, in accents stronger,
As a sense of reason gave it power to make its rhetoric good.

Well I knew that voice—it was an earl's, of soul that matched his station—
Of a soul complete in lordship—might and right read on his brow:
Very finely courteous—far too proud to doubt his domination
Of the common people,—he atones for grandeur by a bow.

High straight forehead, nose of eagle, cold blue eyes, of less expression
Than resistance, coldly casting off the looks of other men,
As steel, arrows,—unelastic lips, which seem to taste possession,
And be cautious lest the common air should injure or distrain.

For the rest, accomplished, upright,—ay, and standing
by his order
With a bearing not ungraceful; fond of arts, and
letters too;
Just a good man, made a proud man,—as the sandy
rocks that border
A wild coast, by circumstances, in a regnant ebb and
flow.

Thus, I knew that voice—I heard it—and I could not
help the hearkening:
In the room I stood up blindly, and my burning heart
within
Seemed to seethe and fuse my senses, till they ran on
all sides, darkening,
And scorched, weighed, like melted metal, round my
feet that stood therein.

And that voice, I heard it pleading, for love's sake—
for wealth, position, . .
For the sake of liberal uses, and great actions to be
done—
And she answered, answered gently—" Nay, my lord,
the old tradition
Of your Normans, by some worthier hand than mine
is, should be won."

" Ah, that white hand!" he said quickly,—and in his
he either drew it,
Or attempted—for with gravity and instance she
replied—

"Nay, indeed, my lord, this talk is vain, and we had best eschew it,
And pass on, like friends, to other points, less easy to decide."

What he said again, I know not. It is likely that his trouble
Worked his pride up to the surface, for she answered in slow scorn—
"And your lordship judges rightly. Whom I marry, shall be noble,
Ay, and wealthy. I shall never blush to think how he was born."

There, I maddened! her words stung me! Life swept through me into fever,
And my soul sprang up astonished; sprang, full-statured in an hour:
Know you what it is when anguish, with apocalyptic NEVER,
To a Pythian height dilates you,—and despair sublimes to power?

From my brain, the soul-wings budded!—waved a flame about my body,
Whence conventions coiled to ashes: I felt self-drawn out, as man,
From amalgamate false natures; and I saw the skies grow ruddy
With the deepening feet of angels, and I knew what spirits can.

I was mad—inspired—say either! anguish worketh inspiration!
Was a man, or beast—perhaps so; for the tiger roars, when speared;
And I walked on, step by step, along the level of my passion—
Oh my soul! and passed the doorway to her face, and never feared.

He had left her,—peradventure, when my footstep proved my coming—
But for *her*—she half arose, then sat—grew scarlet and grew pale:
Oh, she trembled!—'tis so always with a worldly man or woman,
In the presence of true spirits—what else *can* they do but quail?

Oh, she fluttered like a tame bird, in among its forest-brothers,
Far too strong for it! then drooping, bowed her face upon her hands—
And I spake out wildly, fiercely, brutal truths of her and others!
I, she planted in the desert, swathed her, windlike, with my sands.

I plucked up her social fictions, bloody-rooted, though leaf-verdant,
Trod them down with words of shaming,—all the purples and the gold,

And the 'landed stakes' and Lordships—all that spirits pure and ardent
Are cast out of love and reverence, because chancing not to hold.

"For myself I do not argue," said I, "though I love you, Madam,
But for better souls, that nearer to the height of yours have trod—
And this age shows, to my thinking, still more infidels to Adam,
Than directly, by profession, simple infidels to God.

"Yet, O God," (I said,) "O grave," (I said,) "O mother's heart and bosom,
With whom first and last are equal, saint and corpse and little child!
We are fools to your deductions, in these figments of heart-closing!
We are traitors to your causes, in these sympathies defiled!

"Learn more reverence, Madam, not for rank or wealth—*that* needs no learning;
That comes quickly—quick as sin does! ay, and often works to sin;
But for Adam's seed, MAN! Trust me, 'tis a clay above your scorning,
With God's image stamped upon it, and God's kindling breath within.

"What right have you, Madam, gazing in your shining mirror daily,
Getting, so, by heart, your beauty, which all others must adore,—
While you draw the golden ringlets down your fingers, to vow gayly,
You will wed no man that's only good to God,—and nothing more.

"Why, what right have you, made fair by that same God—the sweetest woman
Of all women He has fashioned—with your lovely spirit face,
Which would seem too near to vanish, if its smiles were not so human,—
And your voice of holy sweetness, turning common words to grace:

"What right *can* you have, God's other works, to scorn, despise, ... revile them
In the gross, as mere men, broadly—not as *noble* men, forsooth,—
But as Parias of the outer world, forbidden to assoil them,
In the hope of living—dying,—near that sweetness of your mouth?

"Have you any answer, Madam? If my spirit were less earthy—
If its instrument were gifted with more vibrant silver strings—

I would kneel down where I stand, and say—'Behold me! I am worthy
Of thy loving, for I love thee! I am worthy as a king.'

"As it is—your ermined pride, I swear, shall feel this stain upon her—
That *I*, poor, weak, tost with passion, scorned by me and you again,
Love you, Madam—dare to love you—to my grief and your dishonor—
To my endless desolation, and your impotent disdain!"

More mad words like these—more madness! friend, I need not write them fuller;
And I hear my hot soul dropping on the lines in showers of tears—
Oh, a woman! friend, a woman! Why, a beast had scarce been duller,
Than roar bestial loud complaints against the shining of the spheres.

But at last there came a pause. I stood all vibrating with thunder,
Which my soul had used. The silence drew her face up like a call.
Could you guess what word she uttered? She looked up, as if in wonder,
With tears beaded on her lashes, and said "Bertram!" it was all.

If she had cursed me—and she might have—or if even, with queenly bearing,
Which at need is used by women, she had risen up and said,
" Sir, you are my guest, and therefore, I have given you a full hearing—
Now, beseech you, choose a name exacting somewhat less instead "—

I had borne it!—but that " Bertram "—why it lies there on the paper
A mere word, without her accent,—and you cannot judge the weight
Of the calm which crushed my passion! I seemed swimming in a vapor,—
And her gentleness did shame me, whom her scorn made desolate.

So, struck backward, and exhausted with that inward flow of passion
Which had passed, in deadly rushing, into forms of abstract truth,—
With a logic agonizing through unfit denunciation,—
And with youth's own anguish turning grimly gray the hairs of youth,—

With the sense accursed and instant, that if even I spake wisely,
I spake basely—using truth,—if what I spake, indeed, was true—

To avenge wrong on a woman—*her*, who sat there weighing nicely
A full manhood's worth, found guilty of such deeds as I could do!—

With such wrong and wo exhausted—what I suffered and occasioned,—
As a wild horse, through a city, runs with lightning in his eyes,
And then dashing at a church's cold and passive wall, impassioned,
Strikes the death into his burning brain, and blindly drops and dies—

So I fell, struck down before her! Do you blame me, friend, for weakness?
'Twas my strength of passion slew me!—fell before her like a stone;
Fast the dreadful world rolled from me, on its roaring wheels of blackness!
When the light came I was lying in this chamber—and alone.

Oh, of course, she charged her lacqueys to bear out the sickly burden,
And to cast it from her scornful sight—but not *beyond* the gate—
She is too kind to be cruel, and too haughty not to pardon
Such a man as I—'t were something to be level to her hate.

But for *me*—you now are conscious why, my friend, I write this letter,—
How my life is read all backward, and the charm of life undone!
I shall leave this house at dawn—I would to-night, if I were better—
And I charge my soul to hold my body strengthened for the sun.

When the sun has dyed the orient, I depart with no last gazes,
No weak moanings—one word only left in writing for her hands,—
Out of reach of her derisions, and some unavailing praises,
To make front against this anguish in the far and foreign lands.

Blame me not, I would not squander life in grief—I am abstemious:
I but nurse my spirit's falcon, that its wing may soar again:
There's no room for tears of weakness, in the blind eyes of a Phemius:
Into work the poet kneads them,—and he does not die *till then*.

CONCLUSION.

Bertram finished the last pages, while along the silence ever
Still in hot and heavy splashes, fell his tears on every leaf:
Having ended, he leans backward in his chair, with lips that quiver
From the deep unspoken, ay, and deep unwritten thoughts of grief.

Soh! how still the lady standeth! 'tis a dream—a dream of mercies!
'Twixt the purple lattice-curtains, how she standeth still and pale!
'Tis a vision, sure, of mercies, sent to soften his self-curses—
Sent to sleep a patient quiet, o'er the tossing of his wail.

" Eyes," he said, " now throbbing through me! are ye eyes that did undo me?
Shining eyes, like antique jewels set in Parian statue-stone!
Underneath that calm white forehead, are ye ever burning torrid,
O'er the desolate sand-desert of my heart and life undone?"

With a murmurous stir, uncertain, in the air, the purple curtain
Swelleth in and swelleth out around her motionless pale brows;
While the gliding of the river sends a rippling noise for ever,
Through the open casement whitened by the moonlight's slant repose.

Said he—"Vision of a lady! stand there silent, stand there steady!
Now I see it plainly, plainly; now I cannot hope or doubt—
There, the cheeks of calm expression—there, the lips of silent passion,
Curvéd like an archer's bow to send the bitter arrows out."

Ever, evermore the while in a slow silence she kept smiling,—
And approached him slowly, slowly, in a gliding measured pace;
With her two white hands extended, as if praying one offended,
And a look of supplication, gazing earnest in his face.

Said he—"Wake me by no gesture,—sound of breath, or stir of vesture;
Let the blessed apparition melt not yet to its divine!

No approaching—hush! no breathing! or my heart
must swoon to death in
That too utter life thou bringest—O thou dream of
Geraldine!"

Ever, evermore the while in a slow silence she kept
smiling—
But the tears ran over lightly from her eyes, and
tenderly;
"Dost thou, Bertram, truly love me? Is no woman
far above me,
Found more worthy of thy poet-heart, than such a
one as *I?*"

Said he—"I would dream so ever, like the flowing of
that river,
Flowing ever in a shadow, greenly onward to the
sea;
So, thou vision of all sweetness—princely to a full
completeness,—
Would my heart and life flow onward—deathward—
through this dream of THEE!"

Ever, evermore the while in a slow silence she kept
smiling,—
While the silver tears ran faster down the blushing
of her cheeks;
Then with both her hands enfolding both of his, she
softly told him,
"Bertram, if I say I love thee, . . . 't is the vision
only speaks."

Softened, quickened to adore her, on his knee he fell before her—
And she whispered low in triumph—"It shall be as I have sworn!
Very rich he is in virtues,—very noble—noble, certes;
And I shall not blush in knowing, that men call him lowly born!"

A VISION OF POETS.

"O Sacred Essence, lighting me this hour,
How may I lightly stile thy great power?
Echo. Power.
Power! but of whence? under the greenwood spraye?
Or liv'st in Heaven? saye.
Echo. in Heavens aye.
In Heavens aye! tell, may I it obtayne
By alms, by fasting, prayer,—by paine?
Echo. By paine.
Show me the paine, it shall be undergone:
I to mine end will still go on.
Echo. Go on."

BRITANNIA'S PASTORALS.

A POET could not sleep aright,
For his soul kept up too much light
Under his eyelids for the night:

And thus he rose disquieted,
With sweet rhymes ringing through his head,
And in the forest wandered;

Where, sloping up the darkest glades,
The moon had drawn long colonnades,
Upon whose floor the verdure fades

To a faint silver: pavement fair,
The antique wood-nymphs scarce would dare
To footprint o'er, if such were there,

But rather sit by breathlessly,
With tears in their large eyes to see
The consecrated sight. But HE—

The poet—who with spirit-kiss
Familiar, had long claimed for his
Whatever earthly beauty is,

Who also in his spirit bore
A Beauty passing the earth's store,
Walked calmly onward evermore.

His aimless thoughts in metre went,
Like a babe's hand, without intent,
Drawn down a seven-stringed instrument

Nor jarred it with his humour as,
With a faint stirring down the grass,
An apparition fair did pass.

He might have feared another time,
But all things fair and strange did chime
With his thoughts then—as rhyme to rhyme.

An angel had not startled him,
Dropping from Heaven's encyclic rim
To breathe from glory in the Dim—

Much less a lady, riding slow
Upon a palfrey white as snow,
As smooth as a snow-cloud could go.

Full upon his she turned her face,—
"What, ho, sir poet! dost thou pace
Our woods at night, in ghostly chase

"Of some fair Dryad of old tales,
Who chants between the nightingales,
And over sleep by song prevails?"

She smiled; but he could see arise
Her soul from far adown her eyes,
Prepared as if for sacrifice.

She looked a queen who seemeth gay
From royal grace alone: "Now, nay,"
He answered,—"slumber passed away,

Compelled by instincts in my head,
That I should see to-night instead
Of a fair nymph, some fairer Dread."

She looked up quickly to the sky
And spake:—"The moon's regality
Will hear no praise! she is as I.

"She is in heaven, and I on earth
This is my kingdom—I come forth
To crown all poets to their worth."

He brake in with a voice that mourned—
"To their worth, lady! They are scorned
By men they sing for, till inurned.

"To their worth! Beauty in the mind
Leaves the hearth cold; and love-refined
Ambitions make the world unkind.

"The boor who ploughs the daisy down,
The chief, whose mortgage of renown,
Fixed upon graves, has bought a crown—

"Both these are happier, more approved
Than poets!—Why should I be moved
In saying both are more beloved?"

"The south can judge not of the north;"
She resumed calmly—"I come forth
To crown all poets to their worth.

"Yea, sooth! and to anoint them all
With blessed oils, which surely shall
Smell sweeter as the ages fall."

"As sweet," the poet said, and rung
A low sad laugh, "as flowers do, sprung
Out of their graves when they die young:

"As sweet as window eglantine—
Some bough of which, as they decline,
The hired nurse plucketh at their sign:

"As sweet, in short, as perfumed shroud,
Which the fair Roman maidens sewed
For English Keats, singing aloud."

The lady answered, "Yea, as sweet!
The things thou namest being complete
In fragrance, as I measure it.

"Since sweet the death-clothes and the knell
Of him who, having lived, dies well,—
And holy sweet the asphodel,

"Stirred softly by that foot of his,
When he treads brave on all that is,
Into the world of souls, from this!

"Since sweet the tears, dropped at the door
Of tearless Death,—and even before:
Sweet, consecrated evermore!

"What! dost thou judge it a strange thing,
That poets, crowned for vanquishing,
Should bear some dust from out the ring?

"Come on with me, come on with me;
And learn in coming! Let me free
Thy spirit into verity."

She ceased: her palfrey's paces sent
No separate noises as she went,—
'Twas a bee's hum—a little spent.

And while the poet seemed to tread
Along the drowsy noise so made,
The forest heaved up overhead

Its billowy foliage through the air,
And the calm stars did, far and fair,
O'er-swim the masses everywhere:

Save where the overtopping pines
Did bar their tremulous light with lines
All fixed and black. Now the moon shines

A broader glory. You may see
The trees grow rarer presently,—
The air blows up more fresh and free:

Until they come from dark to light,
And from the forest to the sight
Of the large Heaven-heart, bare with night,—

A fiery throb in every star,
With burning arteries that are
The conduits of God's life afar,—

A wild brown moorland underneath,
Low glimmering here and thither, with
White pools in breaks, as blank as death.

Beside the first pool, near the wood,
A dead tree in set horror stood,
Peeled and disjointed, stark as rood;

Since thunder stricken, years ago,
Fixed in the spectral strain and throe
Wherewith it struggled from the blow:

A monumental tree . . . alone,
That will not bend, if tempest-blown,
But break off sudden like a stone,—

Its lifeless shadow lies oblique
Upon the pool,—where, javelin-like,
The star-rays quiver while they strike.

"Drink," said the lady, very still—
"Be holy and cold." He did her will,
And drank the starry water chill.

The next pool they came near unto,
Was bare of trees: there, only grew
Straight flags and lilies fair to view,

Which sullen on the water sat,
And leant their faces on the flat,
As weary of the starlight-state.

"Drink," said the lady, grave and slow,
"World's use behoveth thee to know."
He drank the bitter wave below.

The third pool, girt with thorny bushes,
And flaunting weeds, and reeds and rushes
That winds sang through in mournful gushes,

Was whitely smeared in many a round
By a slow slime: the starlight swound
Over the ghastly light it found.

"Drink," said the lady, sad and slow—
"World's love behoveth thee to know."
He looked to her, commanding so.

Her brow was troubled, but her eye
Struck clear to his soul. For all reply
He drank the water suddenly,—

Then, with a deathly sickness, passed
Beside the fourth pool and the last,
Where weights of shadow were down-cast

From yew and cypress, and from trails
Of hemlock clasping the trunk-scales,
And flung across the intervals

From yew to yew. Who dareth stoop
Where those moist branches overdroop
Into his heart the chill strikes up:

He hears a silent, gliding coil—
The snakes breathe hard against the soil—
His foot slips in their slimy oil:

And toads seem crawling on his hand,
And clinging bats, but dimly scanned,
Right in his face their wings expand.

A paleness took the poet's cheek;
"Must I drink *here?*" he questioned meek
The lady's will, with utterance weak.

"Ay, ay," she said, "it so must be"—
(And this time she spake cheerfully)
"Behoves thee know world's cruelty."

He bowed his forehead till his mouth
Curved in the wave, and drank unloth,
As if from rivers of the south.

His lip sobbed through the water rank,
His heart paused in him while he drank,
His brain beat heart-like—rose and sank,

And he swooned backward to a dream,
Wherein he lay 'twixt gloom and gleam,
With Death and Life at each extreme.

And spiritual thunders, born of soul
Not cloud, did leap from mystic pole,
And o'er him roll and counter-roll,

Crushing their echoes reboant
With their own wheels. Did Heaven so grant
His spirit a sign of covenant?

At last came silence. A slow kiss
Did crown his forehead after this:
His eyelids flew back for the bliss.

The lady stood beside his head,
Smiling a thought, with hair dispread:
The moonshine seemed dishevelled

In her sleek tresses manifold;
Like Danae's in the rain of old,
That dripped with melancholy gold:

But SHE was holy, pale, and high—
As one who saw an ecstasy
Beyond a foretold agony.

"Rise up!" said she, with voice where song
Eddied through speech—"rise up! be strong;
And learn how right avengeth wrong."

The poet rose up on his feet:
He stood before an altar set
For sacrament, with vessels meet,

And mystic altarlights which shine
As if their flames were crystaline
Carved flames that would not shrink or pine.

The altar filled the central place
Of a great church, and toward its face
Long aisles did shoot and interlace.

And from it a continuous mist
Of incense (round the edges kissed
By a pure light of amethyst)

Wound upward slowly and throbbingly,
Cloud within cloud, right silverly,
Cloud above cloud, victoriously,

Broke full of against the arched roof,
And, thence refracting, eddied off,
And floated through the marble woof

Of many a fine-wrought architrave,—
Then, poising the white masses brave,
Swept solemnly down aisle and nave.

And now in dark, and now in light,
The countless columns, glimmering white,
Seemed leading out to Infinite.

Plunged half-way up the shaft they showed,
In the pale shifting incense-cloud
Which flowed them by, and overflowed,

Till mist and marble seemed to blend,
And the whole temple, at the end,
With its own incense to distend;

The arches, like a giant's bow,
To bend and slacken,—and below
The niched saints to come and go.

Alone, amid the shifting scene,
That central altar stood serene
In its clear steadfast taper-sheen.

Then first, the poet was aware
Of a chief angel standing there
Before that altar, in the glare.

His eyes were dreadful, for you saw
That *they* saw God—his lips and jaw,
Grand-made and strong, as Sinai's Law

They could enunciate, and refrain
From vibratory after-pain ;
And his brow's height was sovereign—

On the vast background of his wings
Arose his image : and he flings,
From each plumed arc, pale glitterings

And fiery flakes (as beateth more
Or less, the angel-heart) before,
And round him, upon roof and floor,

Edging with fire the shifting fumes :
While at his side, 't wixt lights and glooms,
The phantasm of an organ booms.

Extending from which instrument
And angel, right and left-way bent,
The poet's sight grew sentient

Of a strange company around
And toward the altar,—pale and crowned,
With sovran eyes of depth profound.

Deathful their faces were ; and yet
The power of life was in them set—
Never forgot, nor to forget.

Sublime significance of mouth,
Dilated nostril full of youth,
And forehead royal with the truth.

These faces were not multiplied
Beyond your count, but side by side
Did front the altar, glorified :

Still as a vision, yet exprest
Full as an action—look and geste
Of buried saint, in risen rest:

The poet knew them. Faint and dim
His spirit seemed to sink in him,
Then, like a dolphin, change and swim

The current—These were poets true
Who died for Beauty, as martyrs do
For truth—the ends being scarcely two.

God's prophets of the Beautiful
These poets were—of iron rule,
The ruggid cilix, serge of wool.

Here Homer, with the broad suspense
Of thunderous brows, and lips intense
Of garrulous god-innocence.

There, Shakspeare! on whose forehead climb
The crowns o' the world! Oh, eyes sublime—
With tears and laughters for all time!

Here, Æschylus,—the women swooned
To see so awful when he frowned
As the gods did,—he standeth crowned.

Euripides, with close and mild
Scholastic lips,—that could be wild,
And laugh or sob out like a child

Right in the classes. Sophocles,
With that king's look which down the trees,
Followed the dark effigies

Of the lost Theban: Hesiod old,
Who somewhat blind and deaf and cold,
Cared most for gods and bulls. And bold

Electric Pindar, quick as fear,
With race-dust on his cheeks, and clear,
Slant startled eyes that seem to hear

The chariot rounding the last goal,
To hurtle past it in his soul:
And Sappho crowned with aureole

Of ebon curls on calmed brows—
O poet-woman! none foregoes
The leap, attaining the repose!

Theocritus, with glittering locks
Dropt sideway, as betwixt the rocks
He watched the visionary flocks:

And Aristophanes: who took
The world with mirth, and laughter-struck
The hollow caves of Thought and woke

The infinite echoes hid in each.
And Virgil: shade of Mantuan beech
Did help the shade of bay to reach

And knit around his forehead high:—
For his gods wore less majesty
Than his brown bees hummed deathlessly.

Lucretius—nobler than his mood:
Who dropped his plummet down the broad
Deep universe, and said 'No God,'

Finding no bottom: he denied
Divinely the Divine, and died
Chief poet on the Tiber-side,

By grace of God! his face is stern,
As one compelled, in spite of scorn,
To teach a truth he could not learn.

An Ossian, dimly seen or guessed:
Once counted greater than the rest,
When mountain-winds blew out his vest.

And Spenser drooped his dreaming head
(With languid sleep-smile you had said
From his own verse engendered)

On Ariosto's, till they ran
Their locks in one:—The Italian
Shot nimbler heat of bolder man

From his fine lids. And Dante stern
And sweet, whose spirit was an urn
For wine and milk poured out in turn.

Hard-souled Alfieri; and fancy-willed
Boiardo,—who with laughters filled
The pauses of the jostled shield.

And Berni, with a hand stretched out
To sleek that storm: And not without
The wreath he died in, and the doubt

He died by, Tasso: bard and lover,
Whose visions were too thin to cover
The face of a false woman over.

And soft Racine,—and grave Corneille—
The orator of rhymes, whose wail
Scarce shook his purple! And Petrarch pale,

Who from his brainlit heart hath thrown
A thousand thoughts beneath the sun,
Each perfumed with the name of One.

And Camoens, with that look he had,
Compelling India's Genius sad
From the wave through the Lusiad,

With murmurs of a purple ocean
Indrawn in vibrative emotion
Along the verse! And while devotion

In his wild eyes fantastic shone
Between the bright curls blown upon
By airs celestial, . . . Calderon:

And bold De Vega,—who breathed quick
Song after song, till death's old trick
Put pause to life and rhetoric.

And Goethe—with that reaching eye
His soul reached out from, far and high,
And fell from inner entity.

And Schiller, with heroic front
Worthy of Plutarch's kiss upon 't—
Too large for wreath of modern wont.

And Chaucer, with his infantine
Familiar clasp of things divine—
That mark upon his lip is wine.

Here Milton's eyes strike piercing-dim :
The shapes of suns and stars did swim
Like clouds from them, and granted him

God for sole vision ! Cowley, there,
Whose active fancy debonaire
Drew straws like amber—foul to fair.

Drayton and Browne,—with smiles they drew
From outward Nature, to renew
From their own inward nature true.

And Marlowe, Webster, Fletcher, Ben—
Whose fire-heart sowed our furrows, when
The world was worthy of such men.

And Burns, with pungent passionings
Set in his eyes. Deep lyric springs
Are of the fire-mount's issuings.

And Shelley, in his white ideal,
All statue blind ; and Keats, the real
Adonis, with the hymeneal

Fresh vernal buds half sunk between
His youthful curls, kissed straight and sheen
In his Rome-grave, by Venus queen.

And poor, proud Byron,—sad as grave
And salt as life : forlornly brave,
And quivering with the dart he drave.

And visionary Coleridge, who
Did sweep his thoughts as angels do
Their wings, with cadence up the Blue.

These poets faced (and other more)
The lighted altar booming o'er
The clouds of incense dim and hoar:

And all their faces, in the lull
Of natural things, looked wonderful
With life and death and deathless rule:

All still as stone, and yet intense;
As if by spirit's vehemence
That stone were carved, and not by sense.

All still and calm as statue-stone:
The life lay coiled unforgone
Up in the awful eyes alone,

And flung its length out through the air
Into whatever eyes should dare
To front them—Awful shapes and fair!

But where the heart of each should beat,
There seemed a wound instead of it,
From whence the blood dropped to their feet,

Drop after drop—dropped heavily
As century follows century
Into the deep eternity.

Then said the lady,—and her word
Came distant,—as wide waves were stirred
Between her and the ear that heard:—

"World's use is cold—world's love is vain,—
World's cruelty is bitter bane;
But pain is not the fruit of pain.

"Hearken, O poet, whom I led
From the dark wood! Dismissing dread,
Now hear this angel in my stead:

"His organ's pedals strike along
These poets' hearts, which metal-strong,
They gave him without count of wrong,—

"From which foundation he can guide
Up to God's feet, from these who died,
An anthem fully glorified:

"Whereat God's blessing . . . . IBARAK (יברך)
Breathes back this music—folds it back
About the earth in vapory rack:

"And men walk in it, crying 'Lo!
'The world is wider, and we know
'The very heavens look brighter so:

"'The stars move statelier round the edge
'O' the silver spheres, and give in pledge
'Their light for nobler privilege.

"'No little flower but joys or grieves—
'Full life is rustling in the sheaves;
'Full spirit sweeps the forest-leaves:'

"So works this music on the earth:
God so admits it, sends it forth,
To add another worth to worth—

"A new creation-bloom that rounds
The old creation, and expounds
His Beautiful in tuneful sounds.

"Now hearken!" Then the poet gazed
Upon the angel glorious-faced,
Whose hand, majestically raised,

Floated across the organ-keys,
Like a pale moon o'er murmuring seas,
With no touch but with influences.

Then rose and fell (with swell and swound
Of shapeless noises wandering round
A concord which at last they found)

Those mystic keys—the tones were mixed,
Dim, faint; and thrilled and throbbed betwixt
The incomplete and the unfixed:

And therein mighty minds were heard
In mighty musings, inly stirred,
And struggling outward for a word.

Until these surges, having run
This way and that, gave out as one
An Aphrodite of sweet tune,—

A Harmony that, finding vent,
Upward in grand ascension went,
Winged to a heavenly argument—

Up, upward! like a saint who strips
The shroud back from his eyes and lips,
And rises in apocalypse:

A Harmony sublime and plain,
Which cleft (as flying swan, the rain,—
Throwing the drops off with a strain

Of her white wings) those undertones
Of pèrplext chords, and soared at once,
And struck out from the starry thrones

Their several silver octaves, as
It passed to God: The music was
Of divine stature—strong to pass:

And those who heard it, understood
Something of life in spirit and blood—
Something of Nature's fair and good.

And while it sounded, those great souls
Did thrill as racers at the goals,
And burn in all their aureoles.

But she, the lady, as vapor-bound,
Stood calmly in the joy of sound,—
Like nature with the showers around.

And when it ceased, the blood which fell,
Again, alone grew audible,
Tolling the silence as a bell.

The sovran angel lifted high
His hand and spake out sovranly—
"Tried poets, hearken and reply!

"Give me true answers. If we grant
That not to suffer, is to want
The conscience of the Jubilant,—

"If ignorance of anguish is
But ignorance; and mortals miss
Far prospects, by a level bliss,—

"If as two colors must be viewed
In a seen image, mortals should
Need good and evil, to see good,—

"If to speak nobly, comprehends
To feel profoundly—if the ends
Of power and suffering, Nature blends,—

"If poets on the tripod must
Writhe like the Pythian, to make just
Their oracles, and merit trust,—

"If every vatic word that sweeps
To change the world, must pale their lips,
And leave their own souls in eclipse—

"If to search deep the universe
Must pierce the searcher with the curse,—
Because that bolt (in man's reverse,)

"Was shot to the heart o' the wood, and lies
Wedged deepest in the best:—if eyes
That look for visions and surprise

"From marshall'd angels, must shut down
Their lids, first, upon sun and moon,
The head asleep upon a stone,—

"If ONE who did redeem you back,
By His own lack, from final lack,
Did consecrate by touch and track

"Those temporal sorrows, till the taste
Of brackish waters of the waste
Is salt with tears He dropt too fast,—

"If all the crowns of earth must wound
With prickings of the thorns He found,—
If saddest sighs swell sweetest sound,—

"What say ye unto this?—refuse
This baptism in salt water?—choose
Calm breasts, mute lips, and labor loose?

"Or, oh ye gifted givers! ye
Who give your liberal hearts to me,
To make the world this harmony,—

Are ye resigned that they be spent
To such world's help?"—
The Spirits bent
Their awful brows and said—"Content!"

Content! it sounded like *Amen*,
Said by a choir of mourning men—
An affirmation full of pain

And patience:—ay, of glorying,
And adoration,—as a king
Might seal an oath for governing.

Then said the angel—and his face
Lightened abroad, until the place
Grew larger for a moment's space,—

The long aisles flashing out in light,
And nave and transept, columns white,
And arches crossed, being clear to sight,

As if the roof were off, and all
Stood in the noon-sun,—"Lo! I call
To other hearts as liberal.

"This pedal strikes out in the air:
My instrument hath room to bear
Still fuller strains and perfecter.

"Herein is room, and shall be room
While Time lasts, for new hearts to come
Consummating while they consume.

"What living man will bring a gift
Of his own heart, and help to lift
The tune?—The race is to the swift!"

So asked the angel. Straight the while,
A company came up the aisle
With measured step and sorted smile;

Cleaving the incense-clouds that rise,
With winking unaccustomed eyes,
And love-locks smelling sweet of spice.

One bore his head above the rest,
As if the world were dispossessed—
And one did pillow chin on breast,

Right languid—an as he should faint:
One shook his curls across his paint,
And moralized on wordly taint.

One, slanting up his face, did wink
The salt rheum to the eyelid's brink,
To think—O gods! or—not to think!

Some trod out stealthily and slow,
As if the sun would fall in snow,
If *they* walked to, instead of fro.

And some with conscious ambling free,
Did shake their bells right daintily
On hand and foot, for harmony.

And some composing sudden sighs,
In attitudes of point-device,
Rehearsed impromptu agonies.

And when this company drew near
The spirits crowned, it might appear
Submitted to a ghastly fear.

As a sane eye in master-passion
Constrains a maniac to the fashion
Of hideous maniac imitation

In the least geste—the dropping low
O' the lid—the wrinkling of the brow,—
Exaggerate with mock and mow,—

So, mastered was that company
By the crowned vision utterly,
Swayed to a maniac mockery.

One dulled his eyeballs, as they ached
With Homer's forehead—though he lacke
An inch of any. And one racked

His lower lip with restless tooth,—
As Pindar's rushing words forsooth
Were pent behind it. One, his smooth

Pink cheeks, did rumple passionate,
Like Æschylus—and tried to prate
On trolling tongue, of fate and fate:

One set her eyes like Sappho's—or
Any light woman's! one forbore
Like Dante, or any man as poor

In mirth, to let a smile undo
His hard shut lips. And one, that drew
Sour humors from his mother, blew

His sunken cheeks out to the size
Of most unnatural jollities,
Because Anacreon looked jest-wise.

So with the rest.—It was a sight
For great world-laughter, as it might
For great world-wrath, with equal right!

Out came a speaker from that crowd,
To speak for all—in sleek and proud
Exordial periods, while he bowed

His knee before the angel—"Thus,
O angel, who hast called for us,
We bring thee service emulous,—

"Fit service from sufficient soul—
Hand-service, to receive world's dole—
Lip-service, in world's ear to roll

"Adjusted concords—soft enow
To hear the wine cups passing, through,
And not too grave to spoil the show.

"Thou, certes, when thou askest more,
O sapient angel, leanest o'er
The window-sill of metaphor.

"To give our hearts up! fie!—That rage
Barbaric, antedates the age:
It is not done on any stage.

"Because your scald or gleeman went
With seven or nine-stringed instrument
Upon his back—must ours be bent?

"We are not pilgrims, by your leave,
No, nor yet martyrs! if we grieve,
It is to rhyme to . . . summer eve.

"And if we labor, it shall be
As suiteth best with our degree,
In after-dinner reverie."

More yet that speaker would have said,—
Poising between his smiles fair fed,
Each separate phrase till finished;

But all the foreheads of those born
And dead true poets flushed with scorn
Betwixt the bay leaves round them worn—

Ay, jetted such brave fire, that they,
The new-come, shrank and paled away,
Like leaden ashes when the day

Strikes on the hearth! A spirit-blast,
A presence known by power, at last
Took them up mutely—they had passed:

And *he*, our pilgrim-poet, saw
Only their places, in deep awe,—
What time the angel's smile did draw

His gazing upward. Smiling on,
The angel in the angel shone,
Revealing glory in benizon.

Till, ripened in the light which shut
The poet in, his spirit mute
Dropped sudden, as a perfect fruit.

He fell before the angel's feet,
Saying—"If what is true is sweet,
In something I may compass it.

"For where my worthiness is poor,
My will stands richly at the door,
To pay short comings evermore.

"Accept me therefore—Not for price,
And not for pride my sacrifice
Is tendered! for my soul is nice,

And will beat down those dusty seeds
Of bearded corn, if she succeeds
In soaring while the covey feeds.

"I soar—I am drawn up like the lark
To its white cloud: So high my mark,
Albeit my wing is small and dark.

"I ask no wages—seek no fame:
Sew me, for shroud round face and name,
God's banner of the oriflamme.

"I only would have leave to loose
(In tears and blood, if so He choose)
Mine inward music out to use.

"I only would be spent—in pain
And loss, perchance—but not in vain,
Upon the sweetness of that strain,—

"Only project, beyond the bound
Of mine own life, so lost and found,
My voice, and live on in its sound,—

"Only embrace and be embraced
By fiery ends,—whereby to waste,
And light God's future with my past."

The angel's smile grew more divine—
The mortal speaking—ay, its shine
Swelled fuller, like a choir-note fine,

Till the broad gloriole, round his brow,
Did vibrate with the light below;
But what he said I do not know.

Nor know I if the man who prayed,
Rose up accepted, unforbade,
From the church-floor where he was laid,—

Nor if a listening life did run
Through the king-poets, glossing down
Their eyes capacious of renown.

My soul, which might have seen, grew blind
By what it looked on: I can find
No certain count of things behind.

I saw alone, dim white and grand
As in a dream, the angel's hand
Stretched forth in gesture of command,

Straight through the haze—And so, as erst
A strain, more noble than the first,
Mused in the organ, and outburst.

With giant march, from floor to roof,
Rose the full notes; now parted off
In pauses massively aloof,

Like measured thunders; now rejoined
In concords of mysterious kind,
Which won together sense and mind:

Now flashing sharp on sharp along,
Exultant, in a mounting throng,—
Now dying off into a song

Fed upon minors,—starry sounds
Moved on free-paced, in silver rounds,
Enlarging liberty with bounds.

And every rhythm that seemed to close,
Survived in confluent underflows,
Symphonious with the next that rose:

Thus the whole strain being multiplied
And greatened,—with its glorified
Wings shot abroad from side to side,—

Waved backward (as a wind might wave
A Brochen mist, and with as brave
Wild roaring) arch and architrave,

Aisle, transept, column, marble wall,—
Then swelling outward, prodigal
Of aspiration beyond thrall.

Soared,—and drew up with it the whole
Of this said vision—as a soul
Is raised by a thought: and as a roll

Of bright devices is unrolled
Still upward, with a gradual gold,—
So rose the vision manifold,

Angel and organ, and the round
Of spirits, solemnized and crowned,—
While the freed clouds of incense wound

Ascending, following in their track
And glimmering faintly, like the rack
O' the moon, in her own light cast back.

And as that solemn Dream withdrew,
The lady's kiss did fall anew
Cold on the poet's brow as dew.

And that same kiss which bound him first
Beyond the senses, now reversed
Its own law, and most subtly pierced

His spirit with the sense of things
Sensual and present. Vanishings
Of glory, with Æolian wings

Struck him and passed: the lady's face
Did melt back in the chrysopras
Of the orient morning sky that was

Yet clear of lark,—and there and so
She melted, as a star might do,
Still smiling as she melted—slow:

Smiling so slow, he seemed to see
Her smile the last thing, gloriously,
Beyond her—far as memory:

Then he looked round: he was alone—
He lay before the breaking sun,
As Jacob at the Bethel stone.

And thought's entangled skein being wound,
He knew the moorland of his swound,
And the pale pools that seared the ground,—

The far wood-pines, like offing ships—
The fourth pool's yew anear him drips—
World's cruelty attaints his lips;

And still he tastes it—bitter still—
Through all that glorious possible
He had the sight of present ill!

Yet rising calmly up and slowly,
With such a cheer as scorneth folly,
And mild delightsome melancholy,

He journeyed homeward through the wood,
And prayed along the solitude,
Betwixt the pines,—" O God, my God!"

The golden morning's open flowings
Did sway the trees to murmurous bowings,—
In metric chant of blessed poems.

And passing homeward through the wood,
He prayed along the solitude,—
'Thou, Poet-God, art great and good!

"And though we must have, and have had
Right reason to be earthly sad,—
Thou, Poet-God, art great and glad."

CONCLUSION.

Life treads on life, and heart on heart—
We press too close in church and mart,
To keep a dream or grave apart.

And I was 'ware of walking down
That same green forest where had gone
The poet-pilgrim. One by one

I traced his footsteps: From the east
A red and tender radiance pressed
Through the near trees, until I guessed

The sun behind shone full and round;
While up the leafiness profound
A wind scarce old enough for sound,

Stood ready to blow on me when
I turned that way; and now and then
The birds sang and brake off again

To shake their pretty feathers dry
Of the dew sliding droppingly
From the leaf-edges, and apply

Back to their song. 'Twixt dew and bird
So sweet a silence ministered,
God seemed to use it for a word

Yet morning souls did leap and run
In all things, as the least had won
A joyous insight of the sun.

And no one looking round the wood
Could help confessing, as he stood,
This Poet-God is glad and good.

But hark! a distant sound that grows!
A heaving, sinking of the boughs—
A rustling murmur, not of those!

A breezy noise, which is not breeze!
And white-clad children by degrees
Steal out in troops among the trees;

Fair little children, morning-bright
With faces grave, yet soft to sight,—
Expressive of restrained delight.

Some plucked the palm-bows within reach,
And others leapt up high to catch
The upper bows, and shake from each

A rain of dew, till, wetted so,
The child who held the branch let go,
And it swang backward with a flow

Of faster drippings. Then I knew
The children laughed—but the laugh flew
From its own chirrup, as might do

A frightened song-bird; and a child
Who seemed the chief, said very mild,
"Hush! keep this morning undefiled."

His eyes rebuked them from calm spheres;
His soul upon his brow appears
In waiting for more holy years.

I called the child to me, and said,
"What are your palms for?"—"To be spread,"
He answered, "on a poet dead.

"The poet died last month; and now
The world, which had been somewhat slow,
In honoring his living brow,

"Commands the palms—They must be strown
On his new marble very soon,
In a procession of the town."

I sighed and said, "Did he foresee
Any such honor?" "Verily
I cannot tell you," answered he.

"But this I know,—I fain would lay
Mine own head down, another day,
As *he* did,—with the fame away.

"A lily, a friend's hand had plucked,
Lay by his death-bed, which he looked
As deep down as a bee had sucked;

"Then, turning to the lattice, gazed
O'er hill and river, and upraised
His eyes, illumined and amazed

"With the world's beauty, up to God,
Re-offering on his iris broad,
The images of things bestowed

"By the chief Poet,—'God!' he cried,
'Be praised for anguish, which has tried;
For beauty, which has satisfied:—

"'For this world's presence, half within
And half without me—sound and scene—
This sense of Being and Having been.

"'I thank Thee that my soul hath room
For Thy grand world! Both guests may come—
Beauty, to soul—Body, to tomb!

"'I am content to be so weak,—
Put strength into the words I speak,
And I am strong in what I seek.

"'I am content to be so bare
Before the archers! everywhere
My wounds being stroked by heavenly air.

"'I laid my soul before Thy feet,
That Images of fair and sweet
Should walk to other men on it.

"'I am content to feel the step
Of each pure Image!—let those keep
To mandragore, who care to sleep.

"'I am content to touch the brink
Of the other goblet, and I think
My bitter drink a wholesome drink.

"'Because my portion was assigned
Wholesome and bitter—Thou art kind
And I am blessed to my mind.

"'Gifted for giving, I receive
The maythorn, and its scent outgive!
I grieve not that I once did grieve.

"'In my large joy of sight and touch
Beyond what others count for such,
I am content to suffer much.

"'*I know*--is all the mourner saith,--
Knowledge by suffering entereth;
And life is perfected by Death!'"

The child spake nobly. Strange to hear,
His infantine soft accents clear,
Charged wrth high meanings, did appear,—

And fair to see, his form and face,—
Winged out with whiteness and pure grace
From the green darkness of the place.

Behind his head a palm-tree grew;
An orient beam, which pierced it through,
Transversely on his forehead drew

The figure of a palm-branch brown,
Traced on its brightness, up and down
In fine fair lines,—a shadow-crown.

Guido might paint his angels so—
A little angel, taught to go,
With holy words to saints below.

Such innocence of action yet
Significance of object met
In his whole bearing strong and sweet.

And all the children, the whole band,
Did round in rosy reverence stand,
Each with a palm-bough in his hand.

"And so he died," I whispered;—"Nay,
Not *so*," the childish voice did say—
"That poet turned him, first, to pray

"In silence; and God heard the rest,
'Twixt the sun's footsteps down the west.
Then he called one who loved him best,

"Yea, he called softly through the room
(His voice was weak yet tender)—'Come,'
He said, 'come nearer! Let the bloom

"'Of Life grow over, undenied,
This bridge of Death, which is not wide—
I shall be soon at the other side.

"'Come, kiss me!' So the one in truth
Who loved him best—in love, not ruth,
Bowed down and kissed him mouth to mouth.

"And, in that kiss of Love, was won
Life's manumission: All was done—
The mouth that kissed last, kissed *alone*

"But in the former, confluent kiss,
The same was sealed, I think, by His,
To words of truth and uprightness."

The child's voice trembled—his lips shook,
Like a rose leaning o'er a brook,
Which vibrates, though it is not struck.

"And who," I asked, a little moved,
Yet curious-eyed, "was this that loved
And kissed him last, as it behooved?"

"*I*," softly said the child; and then,
"*I*," said he louder, once again.
"*His son*,—my rank is among men.

"And now that men exalt his name,
I come to gather palms with them,
That holy Love may hallow Fame.

"He did not die alone; nor should
His memory live so, 'mid these rude
World-praisers—a worse solitude.

"Me, a voice calleth to that tomb,
Where these are strewing branch and bloom,
Saying, *come nearer!*—and I come.

"Glory to God!" resumed he,
And his eyes smiled for victory
O'er their own tears, which I could see

Fallen on the palm, down cheek and chin
"That poet now hath entered in
The place of rest which is not sin.

"And while he rests, his songs, in troops,
Walk up and down our earthly slopes,
Companioned by diviner Hopes."

"But *thou*," I murmured,—to engage
The child's speech farther—"hast an age
Too tender for this orphanage."

"Glory to God—to God!" he saith—
"Knowledge by suffering entereth;
And life is perfected by Death!"

RHYME OF THE DUCHESS MAY.

In the belfry, one by one, went the ringers from the
sun,— *Toll slowly.*
And the oldest ringer said, "Ours is music for the
Dead,
When the rebecks are all done."

Six abeles i' the kirkyard grow, on the northside in a
row,— *Toll slowly.*
And the shadows of their tops, rock across the little
slopes
Of the grassy graves below.

On the south side and the west, a small river runs in
haste,— *Toll slowly.*
And between the river flowing, and the fair green
trees a growing,
Do the dead lie at their rest.

On the east I sate that day, up against a willow
gray:— *Toll slowly.*
Through the rain of willow-branches, I could see the
low hill-ranges,
And the river on its way.

There I sate beneath the tree, and the bell tolled
solemnly, *Toll slowly.*
While the trees and rivers' voices flowed between the
solemn noises,—
Yet death seemed more loud to me.

There, I read this ancient rhyme, while the bell did
all the time *Toll slowly.*
And the solemn knell fell in with the tale of life and
sin,
Like a rhythmic fate sublime.

THE RHYME.

Broad the forest stood (I read) on the hills of Linte-
ged— *Toll slowly.*
And three hundred years had stood, mute adown
each hoary wood,
Like a full heart, having prayed.

And the little birds sang east, and the little birds
sang west,— *Toll slowly.*
And but little thought was theirs, of the silent antique
years,
In the building of their nest.

Down the sun dropt, large and red, on the towers of
Linteged,— *Toll slowly.*
Lance and spearhead on the height, bristling strange
in fiery light,
While the castle stood in shade.

There, the castle stood up black, with the red sun at
its back,— *Toll slowly.*
Like a sullen smouldering pyre, with a top that flickers fire,
When the wind is on its track.

And five hundred archers tall did besiege the castle
wall,— *Toll slowly.*
And the castle, seethed in blood, fourteen days and
nights had stood,
And to night, anears its fall.

Yet thereunto, blind to doom, three months since, a
bride did come,— *Toll slowly.*
One who proudly trod the floors, and softly whispered
in the doors,
"May good angels bless our home."

Oh, a bride of queenly eyes, with a front of constancies,— *Toll slowly.*
Oh, a bride of cordial mouth,—where the untired
smile of youth
Did light outward its own sighs.

'Twas a Duke's fair orphan-girl, and her uncle's
ward, the Earl *Toll slowly.*
Who betrothed her, twelve years old, for the sake of
dowry gold,
To his son Lord Leigh, the churl.

But what time she had made good all her years of
womanhood,— *Toll slowly.*

Unto both those Lords of Leigh, spake she out right
sovranly,
"My will runneth as my blood.

"And while this same blood makes red this same right
hand's veins," she said,— *Toll slowly.*
"'Tis my will, as lady free, not to wed a Lord of
Leigh,
But Sir Guy of Linteged."

The old Earl he smiled smooth, then he sighed for
wilful youth,— *Toll slowly.*
"Good my niece, that hand withal, looketh somewhat
soft and small,
For so large a will, in sooth."

She, too, smiled by that same sign,—but her smile
was cold and fine,— *Toll slowly.*
"Little hand clasps muckle gold; or it were not
worth the hold
Of thy son, good uncle mine!"

Then the young lord jerked his breath, and sware
thickly in his teeth,— *Toll slowly.*
"He would wed his own betrothed, an she loved him
an she loathed,
Let the life come or the death."

Up she rose with scornful eyes, as her father's child
might rise,— *Toll slowly.*
"Thy hound's blood, my lord of Leigh, stains thy
knightly heel," quoth she,
"And he moans not where he lies.

"But a woman's will dies hard, in the hall or on the
sward!— *Toll slowly.*
"By that grave, my lords, which made me orphaned
girl and dowered lady,
I deny you wife and ward."

Unto each she bowed her head, and swept past with
lofty tread,— *Toll slowly.*
Ere the midnight-bell had ceased, in the chapel had
the priest
Blessed her, bride of Linteged.

Fast and fain the bridal train, along the night-storm
rode amain:— *Toll slowly.*
Wild the steeds of lord and serf, struck their hoofs
out on the turf,
In the pauses of the rain.

Fast and fain, the kinsmen's train, along the storm
pursued amain— *Toll slowly.*
Steed on steed-track, dashing off—thickening, doub-
ling hoof on hoof,
In the pauses of the rain.

And the bridegroom led the flight, on his red-roan
steed of might,— *Toll slowly.*
And the bride lay on his arm, still, as if she feared no
harm,
Smiling out into the night.

"Dost thou fear?" he said at last;—"Nay!" she
answered him in haste,— *Toll slowly.*

"Not such death as we could find—only life with one behind—
Ride on fast as fear—ride fast!"

Up the mountain wheeled the steed—girth to ground, and fetlocks spread,— *Toll slowly.*
Headlong bounds, and rocking flanks,—down he staggered—down the banks,
To the towers of Linteged.

High and low the serfs looked out, red the flambeaus tossed about,— *Toll slowly.*
In the courtyard rose the cry—"Live the Duchess and Sir Guy!"
But she never heard them shout.

On the steed she dropt her cheek, kissed his mane and kissed his neck,— *Toll slowly.*
"I had happier died by thee, than lived on a Lady Leigh,"
Were the words which she did speak.

But a three months' joyaunce lay 'twixt that moment and to-day,— *Toll slowly.*
When five hundred archers tall, stand beside the castle wall,
To recapture Duchess May.

And the castle standeth black, with the red sun at its back,— *Toll slowly.*
And a fortnight's siege is done—and, except the Duchess, none
Can misdoubt the coming wrack.

Then the captain, young Lord Leigh, with his eye so
gray of blee,— *Toll slowly.*
And thin lips, that scarcely sheath the cold white
gnashing of his teeth,
Gnashed in smiling, absently,—

Cried aloud—" So goes the day, bridegroom fair of
Duchess May!— *Toll slowly.*
Look thy last upon that sun. If thou seest to-
morrow's one,
'Twill be through a foot of clay.

" Ha, fair bride! Dost hear no sound, save that
moaning of the hound?— *Toll slowly.*
Thou and I have parted troth,—yet I keep my ven-
geance oath,
And the other may come round.

" Ha! thy will is brave to dare, and thy new love
past compare,— *Toll slowly.*
Yet thine old love's falchion brave, is as strong a
thing to have,
As the will of lady fair.

" Peck on blindly, netted dove!—If a wife's name
thee behove, — *Toll slowly.*
Thou shalt wear the same to-morrow, ere the grave
has hid the sorrow
Of thy last ill-mated love.

O'er his fixed and silent mouth, thou and I will call
back troth, — *Toll slowly.*

He shall altar be and priest,—and he will not cry at least
'I forbid you—I am loath!'

"I will wring thy fingers pale, in the gauntlet of my mail,— *Toll slowly.*
'Little hand and muckle gold' close shall lie within my hold,
As the sword did to prevail."

O the little birds sang east, and the little birds sang west,— *Toll slowly.*
O, and laughed the Duchess May, and her soul did put away
All his boasting, for a jest.

In her chamber did she sit, laughing low to think of it,— *Toll slowly.*
"Tower is strong and will is free—thou canst boast, my lord of Leigh,—
But thou boastest little wit."

In her tire-glass gazed she, and she blushed right womanly,— *Toll slowly.*
She blushed half from her disdain—half, her beauty was so plain,
—"Oath for oath, my lord of Leigh!"

Straight she called her maidens in—"Since ye gave me blame herein,— *Toll slowly.*
That a bridal such as mine, should lack gauds to make it fine,
Come and shrive me from that sin.

"It is three months gone to-day, since I gave mine
hand away.— *Toll slowly.*
Bring the gold and bring the gem, we will keep
bride state in them,
While we keep the foe at bay.

"On your arms I loose my hair;—comb it smooth
and crown it fair,— *Toll slowly.*
I would look in purple-pall, from this lattice down
the wall,
And throw scorn to one that's there!"

O, the little birds sang east, and the little birds sang
west,— *Toll slowly.*
On the tower the castle's lord leant in silence on his
sword,
With an anguish in his breast.

With a spirit-laden weight, did he lean down passion-
ate,— *Toll slowly.*
They have almost sapped the wall,—they will enter
there withal,
With no knocking at the gate.

Then the sword he leant upon, shivered—snapped
upon the stone,— *Toll slowly.*
"Sword," he thought, with inward laugh, "ill thou
servest for a staff,
When thy nobler use is done!

"Sword, thy nobler use is done!—tower is lost, and
shame begun;— *Toll slowly.*

If we met them in the breach, hilt to hilt or speech
to speech,
We should die there, each for one.

"If we met them at the wall, we should singly, vainly
fall,— *Toll slowly.*
But if *I* die here alone,—then I die, who am but
one,
And die nobly for them all.

"Five true friends lie for my sake—in the moat and
in the brake,— *Toll slowly.*
Thirteen warriors lie at rest, with a black wound in
the breast,
And not one of these will wake.

"And no more of this shall be!—heart-blood weighs
too heavily— *Toll slowly.*
And I could not sleep in grave, with the faithful and
the brave
Heaped around and over me.

"Since young Clare a mother hath, and young Ralph a
plighted faith,— *Toll slowly.*
Since my pale young sister's cheeks blush like rose
when Ronald speaks,
Albeit never a word she saith—

"These shall never die for me—life-blood falls too
heavily:— *Toll slowly.*
And if *I* die here apart,—o'er my dead and silent
heart
They shall pass out safe and free.

"When the foe hath heard it said—'Death holds Guy of Linteged,'— *Toll slowly.*
"That new corse new peace shall bring; and a blessed, blessed thing,
Shall the stone be at its head.

"Then my friends shall pass out free, and shall bear my memory,— *Toll slowly.*
Then my foes shall sleek their pride, soothing fair my widowed bride,
Whose sole sin was love of me.

"With their words all smooth and sweet, they will front her and entreat:— *Toll slowly.*
And their purple pall will spread underneath her fainting head,
While her tears drop over it.

"She will weep her woman's tears, she will pray her woman's prayers,— *Toll slowly.*
But her heart is young in pain, and her hopes will spring again
By the suntime of her years.

"Ah, sweet May—ah, sweetest grief!—once I vowed thee my belief,— *Toll slowly.*
That thy name expressed thy sweetness,—May of poets, in completeness!
Now my May-day seemeth brief."

All these silent thoughts did swim o'er his eyes grown strange and dim,— *Toll slowly.*

Till his true men in the place, wished they stood there
face to face
With the foe instead of him.

"One last oath, my friends, that wear faithful hearts
to do and dare!— *Toll slowly.*
Tower must fall, and bride be lost!—swear me ser-
vice worth the cost,"
—Bold they stood around to swear.

"Each man clasp my hand, and swear, by the deed
we failed in there,— *Toll slowly.*
Not for vengeance, not for right, will ye strike one
blow to-night!"—
Pale they stood around—to swear.

"One last boon, young Ralph and Clare! faithful
hearts to do and dare! *Toll slowly.*
Bring that steed up from his stall, which she kissed
before you all,—
Guide him up the turret-stair.

"Ye shall harness him aright, and lead upward to
this height!— *Toll slowly.*
Once in love and twice in war, hath he borne me
strong and far,—
He shall bear me far to-night."

Then his men looked to and fro, when they heard
him speaking so,— *Toll slowly.*
—"'Las! the noble heart," they thought,—"he in
sooth is grief-distraught.—
Would, we stood here with the foe!"

But a fire flashed from his eye, 'twixt their thought
and their reply,— *Toll slowly.*
"Have ye so much time to waste! We who ride here,
must ride fast,
As we wish our foes to fly."

They have fetched the steed with care, in the harness
he did wear,— *Toll slowly.*
Past the court and through the doors, across the
rushes of the floors;
But they goad him up the stair.

Then from out her bower-chambère, did the Duchess
May repair,— *Toll slowly.*
"Tell me now what is your need," said the lady, "of
this steed,
That ye goad him up the stair?"

Calm she stood! unbodkined through, fell her dark
hair to her shoe,— *Toll slowly.*
And the smile upon her face, ere she left the tiring-
glass,
Had not time enough to go.

"Get thee back, sweet Duchess May! hope is gone
like yesterday,— *Toll slowly.*
One half-hour completes the breach; and thy lord
grows wild of speech.—
Get thee in, sweet lady, and pray.

"In the east tower, high'st of all,—loud he cries for
steed from stall,— *Toll slowly.*

'He would ride as far,' quoth he, 'as for love and
victory,
Though he rides the castle-wall.'

"And we fetch the steed from stall, up where never
a hoof did fall.— *Toll slowly.*
Wifely prayer meets deathly need! may the sweet
Heavens hear thee plead,
If he rides the castle-wall."

Low she dropt her head, and lower, till her hair coiled
on the floor,— *Toll slowly.*
And tear after tear you heard, fall distinct as any
word
Which you might be listening for.

"Get thee in, thou soft ladie!—here is never a place
for thee!— *Toll slowly.*
Braid thy hair and clasp thy gown, that thy beauty
in its moan
May find grace with Leigh of Leigh."

She stood up in bitter case, with a pale yet steady
face,— *Toll slowly.*
Like a statue thunderstruck, which, though quivering,
seems to look
Right against the thunder-place.

And her foot trod in, with pride, her own tears i' the
stone beside,— *Toll slowly.*
"Go to, faithful friends, go to!—Judge no more what
ladies do,—
No, nor how their lords may ride!"

Then the good steed's rein she took, and his neck did
kiss and stroke :— *Toll slowly.*
Soft he neighed to answer her ; and then followed up
the stair,
For the love of her sweet look.

Oh, and steeply, steeply wound up the narrow stair
around,— *Toll slowly.*
Oh, and closely, closely speeding, step by step beside
her treading,
Did he follow, meek as hound.

On the east tower, high'st of all,—there, where never
a hoof did fall,— *Toll slowly.*
Out they swept, a vision steady,—noble steed and
lovely lady,
Calm as if in bower or stall !

Down she knelt at her lord's knee, and she looked up
silently,— *Toll slowly.*
And he kissed her twice and thrice, for that look
within her eyes,
Which he could not bear to see.

Quoth he, " Get thee from this strife,—and the sweet
saints bless thy life !— *Toll slowly.*
In this hour, I stand in need of my noble red-roan
steed—
But no more of my noble wife."

Quoth she, " Meekly have I done all thy biddings
under sun :— *Toll slowly.*

But by all my womanhood,—which is proved so, true and good,
I will never do this one.

"Now by womanhood's degree, and by wifehood's verity,— *Toll slowly.*
In this hour if thou hast need of thy noble red-roan steed,
Thou hast also need of *me*.

"By this golden ring ye see on this lifted hand pardiè,— *Toll slowly.*
If this hour, on castle-wall, can be room for steed from stall,
Shall be also room for *me*

"So the sweet saints with me be" (did she utter solemnly,)— *Toll slowly.*
"If a man, this eventide, on this castle-wall will ride,
He shall ride the same with *me*."

Oh, he sprang up in the selle, and he laughed out bitter-well,— *Toll slowly.*
"Wouldst thou ride among the leaves, as we used on other eves,
To hear chime a vesper bell?"

She clang closer to his knee—"Ay, beneath the cypress-tree!— *Toll slowly.*
Mock me not; for otherwhere, than along the green-wood fair,
Have I ridden fast with thee!

"Fast I rode, with new-made vows, from my angry
kinsman's house !— *Toll slowly.*
What ! and would you men should reck, that I
dared more for love's sake,
As a bride than as a spouse ?

"What, and would you it should fall, as a proverb,
before all,— *Toll slowly.*
That a bride may keep your side, while through
castlegate you ride,
Yet eschew the castle-wall ?"

Ho ! the breach yawns into ruin, and roars up against
her suing,— *Toll slowly.*
With the inarticulate din, and the dreadful falling in—
Shrieks of doing and undoing !

Twice he wrung her hands in twain ; but the small
hands closed again,— *Toll slowly.*
Back he reined the steed—back, back ! but she
trailed along his track,
With a frantic clasp and strain !

Evermore the foeman pour through the crash of win-
dow and door,— *Toll slowly.*
And the shouts of Leigh and Leigh, and the shrieks
of "kill !" and "flee !"
Strike up clear the general roar,

Thrice he wrung her hands in twain,—but they
closed and clung again,— *Toll slowly.*

Wild she clung, as one, withstood, clasps a Christ upon the rood,
In a spasm of deathly pain.

She clung wild and she clung mute,—with her shuddering lips half-shut,— *Toll slowly.*
Her head fallen as in swound,—hair and knee swept on the ground,—
She clung wild to stirrup and foot.

Back he reined his steed, back-thrown on the slippery coping stone,— *Toll slowly.*
Back the iron hoofs did grind, on the battlement behind,
Whence a hundred feet went down.

And his heel did press and goad on the quivering flank bestrode, *Toll slowly.*
"Friends, and brothers! save my wife!—Pardon, sweet, in change for life,—
But I ride alone to God!"

Straight as if the Holy name did upbreathe her as a flame,— *Toll slowly.*
She upsprang, she rose upright!—in his selle she sat in sight:
By her love she overcame.

And her head was on his breast, where she smiled as one at rest,— *Toll slowly.*
"Ring," she cried, "O vesper-bell, in the beechwood's old chapelle!
But the passing bell rings best."

They have caught out at the rein, which Sir Guy
threw loose—in vain,— *Toll slowly.*
For the horse in stark despair, with his front hoofs
poised in air,
On the last verge, rears amain.

And he hangs, he rocks between—and his nostrils
curdle in,— *Toll slowly.*
And he shivers head and hoof—and the flakes of
foam fall off;
And his face grows fierce and thin!

And a look of human woe, from his staring eyes did
go,— *Toll slowly.*
And a sharp cry uttered he, in a foretold agony
Of the headlong death below,——

And, "Ring, ring,—thou passing-bell," still she cried,
"i' the old chapelle!"— *Toll slowly.*
Then back-toppling, crashing back—a dead weight
flunk out to wrack,
Horse and riders overfell!

Oh, the little birds sang east, and the little birds sang
west,— *Toll slowly.*
And I read this ancient Rhyme, in the kirkyard
while the chime
Slowly tolled for one at rest.

The abeles moved in the sun, and the river smooth
did run,— *Toll slowly.*
And the ancient Rhyme rang strange, with its passion
and its change,
Here, where all done lay undone.

And beneath a willow tree, I a little grave did see,—
Toll slowly.
Where was graved,—"HERE UNDEFILED, LIETH
MAUD, A THREE-YEAR CHILD,
"EIGHTEEN HUNDRED FORTY-THREE."

Then, O Spirits—did I say—ye who rode so fast that
day,— *Toll slowly.*
Did star-wheels and angel-wings, with their holy win-
nowings,
Keep beside you all the way?

Though in passion ye would dash, with a blind and
heavy crash, *Toll slowly.*
Up against the thick-bossed shield of God's judgment
in the field,—
Though your heart and brain were rash,—

Now, your will is all unwilled—now your pulses are
all stilled,— *Toll slowly.*
Now, ye lie as meek and mild (whereso laid) as
Maud the child,
Whose small grave was lately filled.

Beating heart and burning brow, ye are very patient
now,— *Toll slowly.*

And the children might be bold to pluck the kingscups from your mould,
Ere a month had let them grow.

And you let the goldfinch sing, in the alder near, in spring,— *Toll slowly.*
Let her build her nest and sit all the three weeks out on it,
Murmuring not at anything.

In your patience ye are strong; cold and heat ye take not wrong:— *Toll slowly.*
When the trumpet of the angel blows eternity's evangel,
Time will seem to you not long.

Oh, the little birds sang east, and the little birds sang west, *Toll slowly.*
And I said in underbreath,—all our life is mixed with death,—
And who knoweth which is best?

Oh, the little birds sang east, and the little birds sang west,— *Toll slowly.*
And I smiled to think God's greatness flowed around our incompleteness,—
Round our restlessness, His rest.

THE POET AND THE BIRD.

A FABLE.

SAID a people to a poet—"Go out from among us straightway!
 While we are thinking earthly things, thou singest of divine.
There's a little fair brown nightingale, who, sitting in the gateway,
 Makes fitter music to our ear, than any song of thine!"

The poet went out weeping—the nightingale ceased chanting;
 "Now, wherefore, O thou nightingale, is all thy sweetness done?"
"I cannot sing my earthly things, the heavenly poet wanting,
 Whose highest harmony includes the lowest under sun."

The poet went out weeping,—and died abroad, bereft there—
 The bird flew to his grave and died amid a thousand wails!—
And, when I last came by the place, I swear the music left there
 Was only of the poet's song, and not the nightingale's!

THE LOST BOWER.

In the pleasant orchard closes,
'God bless all our gains,' say we;
But 'May God bless all our losses,'
Better suits with our degree.—
Listen gentle—ay, and simple! Listen children on
the knee!

Green the land is where my daily
Steps in jocund childhood played—
Dimpled close with hill and valley,
Dappled very close with shade;
Summer-snow of apple blossoms, running up from
glade to glade.

There is one hill I see nearer,
In my vision of the rest;
And a little wood seems clearer,
As it climbeth from the west,
Sideway from the tree-locked valley, to the airy up-
land crest.

Small the wood is, green with hazels,
And, completing the ascent,
Where the wind blows and sun dazzles,
Thrills, in leafy tremblement;
Like a heart that, after climbing, beateth quickly
through content.

Not a step the wood advances
O'er the open hill-top's bound:

There, in green arrest, the branches
See their image on the ground:
You may walk beneath them smiling, glad with sight and glad with sound.

For you hearken on your right hand,
How the birds do leap and call
In the greenwood, out of sight and
Out of reach and fear of all;
And the squirrels crack the filberts, through their cheerful madrigal.

On your left, the sheep are cropping
The slant grass and daisies pale;
And five apple-trees stand dropping
Separate shadows toward the vale,
Over which, in choral silence, the hills look you their "All hail!"

Far out, kindled by each other,
Shining hills on hills arise;
Close as brother leans to brother,
When they press beneath the eyes
Of some father praying blessings from the gifts of paradise.

While beyond, above them mounted,
And above their woods also,
Malvern hills, for mountains counted
Not unduly, loom a-row—
Keepers of Piers Plowman's visions, through the sunshine and the snow.*

* The Malvern Hills of Worcestershire, are the scene of Langlande's visions, and thus present the earliest classic ground of English poetry.

Yet in childhood little prized I
That fair walk and far survey :
'Twas a straight walk, unadvised by
The least mischief worth a nay—
Up and down—as dull as grammar on the eve of holiday.

But the wood, all close and clenching
Bough in bough and root in root,—
No more sky (for over-branching)
At your head than at your foot,—
Oh, the wood drew me within it, by a glamour past dispute.

Few and broken paths showed through it,
Where the sheep had tried to run,—
Forced, with snowy wool to strew it
Round the thickets, when anon
They with silly thorn-pricked noses, bleated back into the sun.

But my childish heart beat stronger
Than those thickets dared to grow :
I could pierce them ! *I* could longer
Travel on, methought, than so .
Sheep for sheep-paths ! braver children climb and creep where they would go.

And the poets wander, said I,
Over places all as rude !
Bold Rinaldo's lovely lady
Sat to meet him in a wood—
Rosalinda, like a fountain, laughed out pure with solitude.

And if Chaucer had not travelled
Through a forest by a well,
He had never dreamt nor marvelled
At those ladies fair and fell
Who lived smiling without loving, in their island-citadel.

Thus I thought of the old singers,
And took courage from their song,
Till my little struggling fingers
Tore asunder gyve and thong
Of the lichens which entrapped me, and the barrier branches strong.

On a day, such pastime keeping,
With a fawn's heart debonaire,
Under-crawling, overleaping
Thorns that prick and boughs that bear,
I stood suddenly astonished—I was gladdened unaware

From the place I stood in, floated
Back the covert dim and close ;
And the open ground was coated
Carpet-smooth with grass and moss,
And the blue-bell's purple presence signed it worthily across.

Here a linden-tree stood, brightening
All adown its silver rind ;
For as some trees draw the lightning,
So this tree, unto my mind,
Drew to earth the blessed sunshine, from the sky where it was shrined.

Tall the linden-tree, and near it
An old hawthorn also grew;
And wood-ivy like a spirit
Hovered dimly round the two,
Shaping thence that Bower of beauty, which I sing of thus to you.

'Twas a bower for garden fitter,
Than for any woodland wide:
Though a fresh and dewy glitter
Struck it through, from side to side,
Shaped and shaven was the freshness, as by garden-cunning plied.

Oh, a lady might have come there,
Hooded fairly like her hawk,
With a book or lute in summer,
And a hope of sweeter talk,—
Listening less to her own music, than for footsteps on the walk.

But that bower appeared a marvel
In the wildness of the place!
With such seeming art and travail,
Finely fixed and fitted was
Leaf to leaf, the dark-green ivy, to the summit from the base.

And the ivy, veined and glossy,
Was inwrought with eglantine;
And the wild hop fibred closely,
And the large-leaved columbine,
Arch of door and window mullion, did right sylvanly entwine.

Rose-trees, either side the door, were
Growing lythe and growing tall;
Each one set a summer warder
For the keeping of the hall,—
With a red rose, and a white rose, leaning, nodding at the wall.

As I entered—mosses hushing
Stole all noises from my foot;
And a green elastic cushion,
Clasped within the linden's root,
Took me in a chair of silence, very rare and absolute.

All the floor was paved with glory,—
Greenly, silently inlaid,
Through quick motions made before me,
With fair counterparts in shade,
Of the fair serrated ivy-leaves which slanted overhead

" Is such pavement in a palace?"
So I questioned in my thought:
The sun, shining through the chalice
Of the red rose hung without,
Threw within a red libation, like an answer to my doubt.

At the same time, on the linen
Of my childish lap there fell
Two white may-leaves, downward winning
Through the ceiling's miracle,
From a blossom, like an angel, out of sight yet blessing well.

Down to floor and up to ceiling,
Quick I turned my childish face;
With an innocent appealing
For the secret of the place,
To the trees which surely knew it, in partaking of
the grace.

Where's no foot of human creature,
How could reach a human hand?
And if this be work of nature,
Why is nature sudden bland, [derstand.
Breaking off from other wild work? It was hard to un-

Was she weary of rough-doing,
Of the bramble and the thorn?
Did she pause in tender ruing,
Here, of all her sylvan scorn?
Or, in mock of art's deceiving, was the sudden mild-
ness worn?

Or could this same bower (I fancied)
Be the work of Dryad strong;
Who, surviving all that chanced
In the world's old pagan wrong,
Lay hid, feeding in the woodland, on the last true
poet's song?

Or was this the house of fairies,
Left, because of the rough ways,
Unassoiled by Ave Marys
Which the passing pilgrim prays,—
And beyond St. Catherine's chiming, on the blessed
Sabbath days?

So, young muser, I sat listening
To my Fancy's wildest word—
On a sudden, through the glistening
Leaves around a little stirred,
Came a sound, a sense of music, which was rather felt than heard.

Softly, finely, it inwound me—
From the world it shut me in,—
Like a fountain falling round me,
Which with silver waters thin
Clips a little marble Naiad, sitting smilingly within.

Whence the music came, who knoweth?
I know nothing. But indeed
Pan or Faunus never bloweth
So much sweetness from a reed,
Which has sucked the milk of waters, at the oldest riverhead

Never lark the sun can waken
With such sweetness! when the lark,
The high planets overtaking
In the half evanished Dark,
Cast his singing to their singing, like an arrow to the mark.

Never nightingale so singeth—
Oh! she leans on thorny tree,
And her poet-soul she flingeth
Over pain to victory!
Yet she never sings such music,—or she sings it not to me.

Never blackbirds, never thrushes,
Nor small finches sing as sweet,
When the sun strikes through the bushes,
To their crimson clinging feet,
And their pretty eyes look sideways to the summer heavens complete.

If it *were* a bird, it seemed
Most like Chaucer's, which, in sooth,
He of green and azure dreamèd,
While it sat in spirit-ruth
On that bier of a crownèd lady, singing nigh her silent mouth.

If it *were* a bird!—ah, sceptic,
Give me "Yea" or give me "Nay"—
Though my soul were nympholeptic,
As I heard that virëlay,
You may stoop your pride to pardon, for my sin is far away.

I rose up in exaltation
And an inward trembling heat,
And (it seemed) in geste of passion,
Dropped the music to my feet,
Like a garment rustling downwards!—such a silence followed it.

Heart and head beat through the quiet,
Full and heavily, though slower;
In the song, I think, and by it,
Mystic Presences of power
Had up-snatched me to the Timeless, then returned me to the Hour.

In a child-abstraction lifted,
Straightway from the bower I past;
Foot and soul being dimly drifted
Through the greenwood, till, at last,
In the hill-top's open sunshine, I all consciously was cast.

Face to face with the true mountains,
I stood silently and still;
Drawing strength for fancy's dauntings,
From the air about the hill,
And from Nature's open mercies, and most debonair goodwill.

Oh! the golden-hearted daisies
Witnessed there, before my youth,
To the truth of things, with praises
To the beauty of the truth:
And I woke to Nature's real, laughing joyfully for both.

And I said within me, laughing,
I have found a bower to-day,
A green lusus—fashioned half in
Chance, and half in Nature's play—
And a little bird sings nigh it, I will nevermore missay.

Henceforth, *I* will be the fairy
Of this bower, not built by one;
I will go there, sad or merry,
With each morning's benison:
And the bird shall be my harper in the dream-hall I have won.

So I said. But the next morning,
(—Child, look up into my face—
'Ware, oh sceptic, of your scorning!
This is truth in its pure grace;)
The next morning, all had vanished, or my wandering
missed the place.

Bring an oath most sylvan holy,
And upon it swear me true—
By the wind-bells swinging slowly
Their mute curfews in the dew—
By the advent of the snow-drop—by the rosemary
and rue,—

I affirm by all or any,
Let the cause be charm or chance,
That my wandering searches many
Missed the bower of my romance—
That I nevermore upon it, turned my mortal countenance.

I affirm that, since I lost it,
Never bower has seemed so fair—
Never garden-creeper crossed it,
With so deft and brave an air—
Never bird sung in the summer, as I saw and heard
them there.

Day by day, with new desire,
Toward my wood I ran in faith—
Under leaf and over briar—
Through the thickets, out of breath—
Like the prince who rescued Beauty from the sleep as
long as death.

But his sword of mettle clashèd,
And his arm smote strong, I ween;
And her dreaming spirit flashèd
Through her body's fair white screen,—
And the light thereof might guide him up the cedar alleys green.

But for me, I saw no splendor—
All my sword was my child-heart;
And the wood refused surrender
Of that bower it held apart,
Safe as Œdipus's grave-place, 'mid Colone's olives swart.

As Aladdin sought the basements
His fair palace rose upon,
And the four and twenty casements
Which gave answers to the sun; [down.
So, in wilderment of gazing, I looked up, and I looked

Years have vanished since, as wholly
As the little bower did then;
And you call it tender folly
That such thoughts should come again?
Ah! I cannot change this sighing for your smiling, brother-men!

For this loss it did prefigure
Other loss of better good,
When my soul, in spirit-vigor,
And in ripened womanhood,
Fell from visions of more beauty than an arbor in a wood.

I have lost—oh many a pleasure—
Many a hope and many a power—
Studious health and merry leisure—
The first dew on the first flower!
But the first of all my losses was the losing of the bower.

I have lost the dream of Doing,
And the other Dream of Done—
The first spring in the pursuing,
The first pride in the Begun,—
First recoil from incompletion, in the face of what is won—

Exaltations in the far light,
Where some cottage only is—
Mild dejections in the starlight,
Which the sadder-hearted miss;
And the child-cheek blushing scarlet, for the very shame of bliss.

I have lost the sound child-sleeping
Which the thunder could not break;
Something too of the strong leaping
Of the staglike heart awake,
Which the pale is low for keeping in the road it ought to take.

Some respect to social fictions
Hath been also lost by me;
And some generous genuflexions,
Which my spirit offered free
To the pleasant old conventions of our false Humanity.

All my losses did I tell you,
Ye, perchance, would look away;—
Ye would answer me, "Farewell! you
Make sad company to-day;
And your tears are falling faster than the bitter words you say."

For God placed me like a dial
In the open ground, with power;
And my heart had for its trial,
All the sun and all the shower!
And I suffered many losses; and my first was of the [bower.

Laugh ye? If that loss of mine be
Of no heavy seeming weight—
When the cone falls from the pine-tree,
The young children laughed thereat;
Yet the wind that struck it, riseth, and the tempest shall be great!

One who knew me in my childhood,
In the glamour and the game,
Looking on me long and mild, would
Never know me for the same.
Come, unchanging recollections, where those changes overcame.

On this couch I weakly lie on,
While I count my memories,—
Through the fingers which, still sighing,
I press closely on mine eyes,—
Clear as once beneath the sunshine, I behold the bower arise.

Springs the linden-tree as greenly,
Stroked with light adown its rind—
And the ivy-leaves serenely
Each in either intertwined,
And the rose-trees at the doorway, they have neither grown nor pined.

From those overblown faint roses,
Not a leaf appeareth shed,
And that little bud discloses
Not a thorn's-breadth more of red,
For the winters and the summers which have passed me overhead.

And that music overfloweth,
Sudden sweet, the sylvan eaves;
Thrush or nightingale—who knoweth?
Fay and Faunus—who believes?
But my heart still trembles in me, to the trembling of the leaves.

Is the bower lost, then? Who sayeth
That the bower indeed is lost?
Hark! my spirit in it prayeth
Through the solstice and the frost,—
And the prayer preserves it greenly, to the last and uttermost—

Till another open for me
In God's Eden-land unknown,
With an angel at the doorway,
White with gazing at His Throne;
And a saint's voice in the palm-trees, singing—"ALL IS LOST . . . and *won!*"

A CHILD ASLEEP.

How he sleepeth! having drunken
  Weary childhood's mandragore,
From his pretty eyes have sunken
  Pleasures, to make room for more—
Sleeping near the withered nosegay, which he pulled the day before.

Nosegays! leave them for the waking:
  Throw them earthward where they grew:
Dim are such beside the breaking
  Amaranths he looks unto—
Folded eyes see brighter colors than the open ever do.

Heaven-flowers, rayed by shadows golden
  From the palms they sprang beneath
Now perhaps divinely holden,
  Swing against him in a wreath—
We may think so from the quickening of his bloom and of his breath.

Vision unto vision calleth,
  While the young child dreameth on:
Fair, O dreamer, thee befalleth
  With the glory thou hast won!
Darker wert thou in the garden, yestermorn, by summer sun.

We should see the spirits ringing
Round thee,—were the clouds away
'Tis the child-heart draws them, singing
In the silent-seeming clay—
Singing!—Stars that seem the mutest, go in music all the way.

As the moths around a taper,
As the bees around a rose,
As the gnats around a vapor,—
So the spirits group and close
Round about a holy childhood, as if drinking its repose.

Shapes of brightness overlean thee,
With their diadems of youth
On the ringlets which half screen thee
While thou smilest, . . not in sooth
Thy smile, . . but the overfair one, dropt from some ethereal mouth.

Haply it is angels' duty,
During slumber, shade by shade
To fine down this childish beauty
To the thing it must be made,
Ere the world shall bring it praises, or the tomb shall see it fade.

Softly, softly! make no noises!
Now he lieth dead and dumb—
Now he hears the angels' voices
Folding silence in the room—
Now he muses deep the meaning of the Heaven-words as they come.

Speak not! he is consecrated—
Breathe no breath across his eyes:
Lifted up and separated
On the hand of God he lies,
In a sweetness beyond touching,—held in cloistral sanctities.

Could ye bless him—father—mother?
Bless the dimple in his cheek?
Dare ye look at one another,
And the benediction speak?
Would ye not break out in weeping, and confess yourselves too weak?

He is harmless—ye are sinful,—
Ye are troubled,—he, at ease:
From his slumber, virtue winful
Floweth outward with increase—
Dare not bless him! but be blessed by his peace—and go in peace.

THE CRY OF THE CHILDREN.

"Φεῦ, φεῦ, τι προσδερκεσθε μ' ομμασιν, τεκνα."
MEDEA.

Do ye hear the children weeping, O my brothers,
Ere the sorrow comes with years?
They are leaning their young heads against their mothers,—
And *that* cannot stop their tears.
The young lambs are bleating in the meadows:
The young birds are chirping in the nest;
The young fawns are playing with the shadows;
The young flowers are blowing toward the west—
But the young, young children, O my brothers,
They are weeping bitterly!—
They are weeping in the playtime of the others,
In the country of the free.

Do you question the young children in the sorrow,
Why their tears are falling so?—
The old man may weep for his to-morrow
Which is lost in Long Ago—
The old tree is leafless in the forest—
The old year is ending in the frost—
The old wound, if stricken, is the sorest—
The old hope is hardest to be lost:

But the young, young children, O my brothers,
Do you ask them why they stand
Weeping sore before the bosoms of their mothers,
In our happy Fatherland?

They look up with their pale and sunken faces,
And their looks are sad to see,
For the man's grief abhorrent, draws and presses
Down the cheeks of infancy—
"Your old earth," they say, "is very dreary;
Our young feet," they say, "are very weak!
Few paces have we taken, yet are weary—
Our grave-rest is very far to seek:
Ask the old why they weep, and not the children,
For the outside earth is cold,—
And we young ones stand without, in our bewildering,
And the graves are for the old:

"True," say the young children, "it may happen
That we die before our time:
Little Alice died last year—the grave is shapen
Like a snowball, in the rime.
We looked into the pit prepared to take her—
Was no room for any work in the close clay:
From the sleep wherein she lieth none will wake her,
Crying, 'Get up, little Alice! it is day.'
If you listen by that grave, in sun and shower,
With your ear down, little Alice never cries!—
Could we see her face, be sure we should not know her,
For the smile has time for growing in her eyes,—

And merry go her moments, lulled and stilled in
The shroud, by the kirk-chime!
It is good when it happens," say the children,
"That we die before our time!"
Alas, alas, the children! they are seeking
Death in life, as best to have!
They are binding up their hearts away from breaking,
With a cerement from the grave.
Go out, children, from the mine and from the city—
Sing out, children, as the little thrushes do—
Pluck you handfuls of the meadow-cowslips pretty—
Laugh aloud, to feel your fingers let them through!
But they answer, "Are your cowslips of the meadows
Like our weeds anear the mine?
Leave us quiet in the dark of the coal-shadows,
From your pleasures fair and fine!

"For oh," say the children, "we are weary,
And we cannot run or leap—
If we cared for any meadows, it were merely
To drop down in them and sleep.
Our knees tremble sorely in the stooping—
We fall upon our faces, trying to go;
And, underneath our heavy eyelids drooping,
The reddest flower would look as pale as snow.
For, all day, we drag our burden tiring,
Through the coal-dark underground—
Or, all day, we drive the wheels of iron
In the factories, round and round.

"For, all day, the wheels are droning, turning,—
Their wind comes in our faces,—

Till our hearts turn,—our heads, with pulses burning,
    And the walls turn in their places—
Turns the sky in the high window blank and reeling—
  Turns the long light that droppeth down the wall—
Turn the black flies that crawl along the ceiling—
  All are turning, all the day, and we with all!—
And all day the iron wheels are droning;
    And sometimes we could pray,
'O ye wheels,' (breaking out in a mad moaning,)—
    'Stop! be silent for to-day!'"

Ay! be silent! Let them hear each other breathing
    For a moment, mouth to mouth—
Let them touch each other's hands, in a fresh wreathing
    Of their tender human youth!
Let them feel that this cold metallic motion
  Is not all the life God fashions or reveals—
Let them prove their inward souls against the notion
  That they live in you, or under you, O wheels!—
Still, all day, the iron wheels go onward,
    Grinding life down from its mark;
And the children's souls, which God is calling sunward,
    Spin on blindly in the dark.

Now tell the poor young children, O my brothers,
    To look up to Him and pray—
So the blessed One, who blesseth all the others,
    Will bless them another day.
They answer, "Who is God that He should hear us,
  While the rushing of the iron wheels is stirred?

When we sob aloud, the human creatures near us
Pass by, hearing not, or answer not a word!
And *we* hear not (for the wheels in their resounding)
Strangers speaking at the door:
Is it likely God, with angels singing round Him,
Hears our weeping any more?
"Two words, indeed, of praying we remember;
And at midnight's hour of harm,—
'Our Father,' looking upward in the chamber,
We say softly for a charm.*
We know no other words, except 'Our Father,'
And we think that, in some pause of angels' song,
God may pluck them with the silence sweet to gather,
And hold both within His right hand which is strong.
'Our Father!' If He heard us, He would surely
(For they call him good and mild)
Answer, smiling down the steep world very purely,
'Come and rest with me, my child.'

"But, no!" say the children, weeping faster,
"He is speechless as a stone;
And they tell us, of His image is the master
Who commands us to work on.
"Go to!" say the children,—"Up in Heaven,
Dark, wheel-like, turning clouds are all we find:
Do not mock us; grief has made us unbelieving,—
We look up for God, but tears have made us blind."

---

* A fact rendered pathetically historical by Mr. Horne's Report of his commission. The name of the poet of "Orion" and "Cosmo de' Medici" has, however, a change of associations, and comes in time to remind me (with other noble instances) that we have some noble poetic heat still in our literature,—though open to the reproach, on certain points, of being somewhat gelid in our humanity.

Do you hear the children weeping and disproving,
O my brothers, what ye preach?
For God's possible is taught by His world's loving—
And the children doubt of each.

And well may the children weep before you;
They are weary ere they run;
They have never seen the sunshine, nor the glory
Which is brighter than the sun:
They know the grief of man, but not the wisdom;
They sink in man's despair, without its calm—
Are slaves, without the liberty in Christdom,—
Are martyrs, by the pang without the palm,—
Are worn as if with age, yet unretrievingly
No dear remembrance keep,—
Are orphans of the earthly love and heavenly:
Let them weep! let them weep!
They look up, with their pale and sunken faces,
And their look is dread to see,
For they mind you of their angels in their places,
With eyes meant for Deity;—
"How long," they say, "how long, O cruel nation,
Will you stand, to move the world, on a child's heart,—
Stifle down with a mailed heel its palpitation,
And tread onward to your throne amid the mart?
Our blood splashes upward, O our tyrants,
And your purple shows your path;
But the child's sob curseth deeper in the silence
Than the strong man in his wrath!"

CROWNED AND WEDDED.

When last before her people's face her own fair face
she bent,
Within the meek projection of that shade she was
content
To erase the child-smile from her lips, which seemed
as if it might
Be still kept holy from the world, to childhood still in
sight—
To erase it with a solemn vow,—a princely vow—to
rule—
A priestly vow—to rule by grace of God the pitiful,—
A very god-like vow—to rule in right and righteousness,
And with the law and for the land!—so God the vower
bless!
The minster was alight that day, but not with fire, I
ween,
And long-drawn glitterings swept adown that mighty
aisled scene:
The priests stood stoled in their pomp, the sworded
chiefs in theirs,
And so, the collared knights,—and so, the civil minis-
ters,—
And so, the waiting lords and dames—and little pages
best
At holding trains—and legates so, from countries east
and west—

So, alien princes, native peers, and high-born ladies bright,
Along whose brows the queen's new crowned, flashed coronets to light!—
And so, the people at the gates, with priestly hands on high,
Which bring the first anointing to all legal majesty.
And so the DEAD—who lie in rows beneath the minster floor,
There, verily an awful state maintaining evermore—
The statesman, whose clean palm will kiss no bribe whate'er it be—
The courtier, who, for no fair queen, will rise up to his knee—
The court-dame, who, for no court-tire, will leave her shroud behind—
The laureate, who no courtlier rhyme than "dust to dust" can find—
The kings and queens, who having made that vow and worn that crown,
Descended unto lower thrones and darker, deep adown!
Dieu et mon droit—what is't to them?—what meaning can it have?—
The King of kings, the rights of death—God's judgment and the grave!
And when betwixt the quick and dead the young fair queen had vowed,
The living shouted "May she live! Victoria, live!" aloud—
And as the loyal shouts went up, true spirits prayed between,

"The blessings happy monarchs have, be thine, O crowned queen!"
But now before her people's face she bendeth hers anew,
And calls them, while she vows, to be her witness thereunto.
She vowed to rule, and in that oath, her childhood put away—
She doth maintain her womanhood, in vowing love to-day.
O, lovely lady!—let her vow!—such lips become such vows,—
And fairer goeth bridal wreath than crown with vernal brows!
O, lovely lady!—let her vow!—yea, let her vow to love!—
And though she be no less a queen—with purples hung above,
The pageant of a court behind, the royal kin around,
And woven gold to catch her looks turned maidenly to ground,—
Yet may the bride-veil hide from her a little of that state,
While loving hopes, for retinues, about her sweetness wait:—
SHE vows to love, who vowed to rule—the chosen at her side
Let none say, God preserve the queen!—but rather, Bless the bride!—
None blow the trump, none bend the knee, none violate the dream
Wherein no monarch, but a wife, she to herself may seem:

Or, if ye say, Preserve the queen!—oh, breathe it inward low—
She is a *woman* and *beloved!*—and 'tis enough but so!
Count it enough, thou noble prince, who tak'st her by the hand,
And claimest for thy lady-love, our lady of the land!—
And since, Prince Albert, men have called thy spirit high and rare,
And true to truth and brave for truth, as some at Augsburg were,—
We charge thee, by thy lofty thoughts, and by thy poet-mind,
Which not by glory and degree takes measure of mankind,
Esteem that wedded hand less dear for sceptre than for ring,
And hold her uncrowned womanhood to be the royal thing:
And now, upon our queen's last vow, what blessings shall we pray?
None straitened to a shallow crown, will suit our lips to-day.
Behold, they must be free as love—they must be broad as free,
Even to the borders of heaven's light and earth's humanity:
Long live she!—send up loyal shouts—and true hearts pray between,—
"The blessings happy PEASANTS have, be thine, O crowned queen!"

CROWNED AND BURIED.

NAPOLEON!—years ago, and that great word,
Compáct of human breath in hate and dread
And exultation, skied us overhead—
An atmosphere whose lightning was the sword,
Scathing the cedars of the world,—drawn down
In burnings, by the metal of a crown.

Napoleon! Nations, while they cursed that name,
Shook at their own curse; and while others bore
Its sound, as of a trumpet, on before,
Brass-fronted legions justified its fame—
And dying men, on trampled battle-sods,
Near their last silence, uttered it for God's.

Napoleon! Sages, with high foreheads drooped,
Did use it for a problem; children small
Leapt up to greet it, as at manhood's call:
Priests blessed it from their altars overstooped
By meek-eyed Christs,—and widows with a moan
Spake it, when questioned why they sat alone.

That name consumed the silence of the snows
In Alpine keeping, holy and cloud-hid:
The mimic eagles dared what Nature's did,
And over-rushed her mountainous repose
In search of eyries: and the Egyptian river
Mingled the same word with its grand 'For ever.'

That name was shouted near the pyramídal
Egyptian tombs, whose mummied habitants,
Packed to humanity's significance,
Motioned it back with stillness: Shouts as idle
As hireling artists' work of myrrh and spice,
Which swathed last glories round the Ptolemies.

The world's face changed to hear it: Kingly men
Came down, in chidden babes' bewilderment,
From autocratic places—each content
With sprinkled ashes for anointing:—then
The people laughed or wondered for the nonce,
To see one throne a composite of thrones.

Napoleon! And the torrid vastitude
Of India felt, in throbbings of the air,
That name which scattered by disastrous blare
All Europe's bound-lines,—drawn afresh in blood:
Napoleon—from the Russias, west to Spain!
And Austria trembled—till we heard her chain.

And Germany was 'ware—and Italy,
Oblivious of old fames—her laurel-locked,
High-ghosted Cæsars passing uninvoked,—
Did crumble her own ruins with her knee,
To serve a newer:—Ay! and Frenchmen cast
A future from them, nobler than her past.

For, verily, though France augustly rose
With that raised NAME, and did assume by such
The purple of the world,—none gave so much

As she, in purchase—to speak plain, in loss—
Whose hands, to freedom stretched, dropped paralyzed
To wield a sword, or fit an undersized

King's crown to a great man's head. And though along
Her Paris' streets, did float on frequent streams
Of triumph, pictured or emmarbled dreams,
Dreampt right by genius in a world gone wrong,—
No dream, of all so won, was fair to see
As the lost vision of her liberty.

Napoleon! 'twas a high name lifted high!
It met at last God's thunder sent to clear
Our compassing and covering atmosphere,
And open a clear sight, beyond the sky,
Of sùpreme empire: this of earth's was done—
And kings crept out again to feel the sun.

The kings crept out—the peoples sat at home,
And finding the long-invocated peace
A pall embroidered with worn images
Of rights divine, too scant to cover doom
Such as they suffered,—cursed the corn that grew
Rankly, to bitter bread, on Waterloo.

A deep gloom centered in the deep repose—
The nations stood up mute to count their dead—
And *he* who owned the NAME which vibrated
Through silence,—trusting to his noblest foes,
When earth was all too gray for chivalry—
Died of their mercies, 'mid the desert sea.

O wild St. Helen! very still she kept him,
With a green willow for all pyramid,—
Which stirred a little if the low wind did,
A little more, if pilgrims overwept him
Disparting the lithe boughs to see the clay
Which seemed to cover his for judgment-day.

Nay! not so long!—France kept her old affection,
As deeply as the sepulchre the corse,
Until dilated by such love's remorse
To a new angel of the resurrection,
She cried, "Behold, thou England! I would have
The dead whereof thou wottest, from that grave."

And England answered in the courtesy
Which, ancient foes turned lovers, may befit,—
"Take back thy dead! and when thou buriest it,
Throw in all former strifes 'twixt thee and me."
Amen, mine England! 'tis a courteous claim—
But ask a little room too . . . for thy shame!

Because it was not well, it was not well,
Nor tuneful with thy lofty-chanted part
Among the Oceanides,—that heart
To bind and bare, and vex with vulture fell.
I would, my noble England, men might seek
All crimson stains upon thy breast—not cheek!

I would that hostile fleets had scarred thy bay,
Instead of the lone ship which waited moored
Until thy princely purpose was assured,

Then left a *shadow*—not to pass away—
Not for to-night's moon, nor to-morrow's sun!
Green watching hills, ye witnessed what was done!

And since it *was* done,—in sepulchral dust,
We fain would pay back something of our debt
To France, if not to honor, and forget
How through much fear we falsified the trust
Of a fallen foe and exile :—We return
Orestes to Electra . . . in his urn.

A little urn—a little dust inside,
Which once outbalanced the large earth, albeit
To-day, a four-years' child might carry it,
Sleek-browed and smiling, "Let the burden 'bide!"
Orestes to Electra !—O fair town
Of Paris, how the wild tears will run down,

And run back in the chariot-marks of Time,
When all the people shall come forth to meet
The passive victor, death-still in the street
He rode through 'mid the shouting and bell-chime
And martial music,—under eagles which
Dyed their rapacious beaks at Austerlitz.

Napoleon! he hath come again—borne home
Upon the popular ebbing heart,—a sea
Which gathers its own wrecks perpetually,
Majestically moaning. Give him room!—
Room for the dead in Paris! welcome solemn
And grave deep, 'neath the cannon-moulded column!*

* It was the first intention to bury him under the column.

There, weapon spent and warrior spent may rest
From roar of fields: provided Jupiter
Dare trust Saturnus to lie down so near
His bolts!—And this he *may:* For, dispossessed
Of any godship, lies the godlike arm—
The goat, Jove sucked, as likely to do harm.

And yet . . . Napoleon!—the recovered name
Shakes the old casements of the world! and we
Look out upon the passing pageantry,
Attesting that the Dead makes good his claim
To a Gaul grave,—another kingdom won—
The last—of few spans—by Napoleon.

Blood fell like dew beneath his sunrise—sooth!
But glittered dew-like in the covenanted
And high-rayed light. He was a despot—granted!
But the αυτος of his autocratic mouth
Said yea i' the people's French: he magnified
The image of the freedom he denied.

And if they asked for rights, he made reply,
"Ye have my glory!"—and so, drawing round them
His ample purple, glorified and bound them
In an embrace that seemed identity.
He ruled them like a tyrant—true! but none
Were ruled like slaves! Each felt Napoleon!

I do not praise this man: the man was flawed
For Adam—much more, Christ!—his knee, unbent—
His hand, unclean—his aspiration, pent

Within a sword-sweep—pshaw!—but since he had
The genius to be loved, why let him have
The justice to be honored in his grave

I think this nation's tears, poured thus together,
Nobler than shouts: I think this funeral
Grander than crownings, though a Pope bless all:
I think this grave stronger than thrones: But whether
The crowned Napoleon or the buried clay
Be better, I discern not—Angels may.

THE FOURFOLD ASPECT.

When ye stood up in the house
  With your little childish feet,
And, in touching Life's first shows,
  First, the touch of Love, did meet,—
Love and Nearness seeming one,
  By the heart-light cast before,—
And, of all Beloveds, none
  Standing farther than the door—
Not a name being dear to thought,
  With its owner beyond call,—
Nor a face, unless it brought
  Its own shadow to the wall,—
When the worst recorded change
  Was of apple dropt from bough,—
When love's sorrow seemed more strange
  Than love's treason can seem now,—
Then, the Loving took you up
  Soft, upon their elder knees,—
Telling why the statues droop
  Underneath the churchyard trees,—
And how *ye* must lie beneath them,
  Through the winters long and deep,
Till the last trump overbreathe them,
  And ye smile out of your sleep . . .
Oh, ye lifted up your head, and it seemed as if they said

A tale of fairy ships
With a swan-wing for a sail!—
Oh, ye kissed their loving lips
For the merry, merry tale!—
So carelessly ye thought upon the Dead.

Soon ye read in solemn stories
Of the men of long ago—
Of the pale bewildering glories
Shining farther than we know,—
Of the heroes with the laurel,
Of the poets with the bay,
Of the two worlds' earnest quarrel
For that beauteous Helena,—
How Achilles at the portal
Of the tent, heard footsteps nigh,
And his strong heart, half-immortal,
Met the *keitai* with a cry,—
How Ulysses left the sunlight
For the pale eidola race,
Blank and passive through the dun light,
Staring blindly on his face:
How that true wife said to Pœtus,
With calm smile and wounded heart,—
"Sweet, it hurts not!"—how Admetus
Saw his blessed one depart.
How King Arthur proved his mission,—
And Sir Rowland wound his horn,—
And at Sangreal's moony vision
Swords did bristle round like corn.
Oh! ye lifted up your head, and it seemed the while ye read,

That this death, then, must be found
A Valhalla for the crowned—
The heroic who prevail:
None, be sure, can enter in
Far below a paladin
Of a noble, noble tale!—
So, awfully, ye thought upon the Dead.

Ay! but soon ye woke up shrieking,—
As a child that wakes at night
From a dream of sisters speaking
In a garden's summer-light,—
That wakes, starting up and bounding,
In a lonely, lonely bed,
With a wall of darkness round him,
Stifling black about his head!—
And the full sense of your mortal
Rushed upon you deep and loud,
And ye heard the thunder hurtle
From the silence of the cloud—
Funeral-torches at your gateway
Threw a dreadful light within;
All things changed! you rose up straightway,
And saluted Death and Sin:
Since,—your outward man has rallied,
And your eye and voice grown bold—
Yet the Sphinx of Life stands pallid,
With her saddest secret told:
Happy places have grown holy:
If ye went where once ye went,
Only tears would fall down slowly,
As at solemn sacrament:

Merry books, once read for pastime,
  If ye dared to read again,
Only memories of the last time
  Would swim darkly up the brain:
Household *names*, which used to flutter
  Through your laughter unawares,—
God's Divine one, ye could utter
  With less trembling in your prayers!
Ye have dropt adown your head, and it seems as if ye
      tread
  On your own hearts in the path
  Ye are called to in His wrath,—
  And your prayers go up in wail!
  —'Dost Thou see, them, all our loss,
  O Thou agonized on cross?
  Art thou reading all its tale?
So, mournfully, ye think upon the Dead!

Pray, pray, *thou* who also weepest,
  And the drops will slacken so;—
Weep, weep:—and the watch thou keepest,
  With a quicker count will go.
Think:—the shadow on the dial
  For the nature most undone,
Marks the passing of the trial,
  Proves the presence of the sun:
Look, look up, in starry passion,
  To the throne above the spheres,—
Learn: the spirit's gravitation
  Still must differ from the tear's.
Hope: with all the strength thou usest
  In embracing thy despair:

Love : the earthly love thou losest
  Shall return to thee more fair.
Work : make clear the forest-tangles
  Of the wildest stranger-land :
Trust : the blessed deathly angels
  Whisper, 'Sabbath hours at hand !'
By the heart's wound when most gory
  By the longest agony,
Smile !—Behold, in sudden glory
  The TRANSFIGURED smiles on *thee !*
And ye lifted up your head, and it seemed as if He said,
  "My Beloved, is it so ?
  Have ye tasted of my wo ?—
  Of my Heaven ye shall not fail !"—
  He stands brightly where the shade is,
  With the keys of Death and Hades,
  And there, ends the mournful tale :—
So, hopefully, ye think upon the Dead.

A FLOWER IN A LETTER.

My lonely chamber next the sea,
Is full of many flowers set free
  By summer's earliest duty;
Dear friends upon the garden-walk
Might stop amid their fondest talk,
  To pull the least in beauty.

A thousand flowers—each seeming one
That learnt, by gazing on the sun,
  To counterfeit his shining—
Within whose leaves the holy dew
That falls from heaven, hath won anew
  A glory . . . in declining.

Red roses used to praises long,
Contented with the poet's song,
  The nightingale's being over:
And lilies white, prepared to touch
The whitest thought, nor soil it much,
  Of dreamer turned to lover.

Deep violets you liken to
The kindest eyes that look on you,
  Without a thought disloyal:
And cactuses, a queen might don,
If weary of a golden crown,
  And still appear as royal.

Pansies for ladies all! I wis
That none who wear such brooches, miss
A jewel in the mirror:
And tulips, children love to stretch
Their fingers down, to feel in each
Its beauty's secret nearer.

Love's language may be talked with these:
To work out choicest sentences,
No blossoms can be meeter,—
And, such being used in Eastern bowers,
Young maids may wonder if the flowers
Or meanings be the sweeter.

And such being strewn before a bride,
Her little foot may turn aside,
Their longer bloom decreeing;
Unless some voice's whispered sound
Should make her gaze upon the ground
Too earnestly—for seeing.

And such being scattered on a grave,
Whoever mourneth there may have
A type that seemeth worthy
Of a fair body hid below,
Which bloomed on earth a time ago,
Then perished as the earthy.

And such being wreathed for worldly feast,
Across the brimming cup some guest
Their rainbow colors viewing,

May feel them,—with a silent start,—
The covenant, his childish heart
With nature made,—renewing.

No flowers our gardened England hath,
To match with these in bloom and breath,
Which from the world are hiding
In sunny Devon moist with rills,
A nunnery of cloistered hills,
The elements presiding.

By Loddon's stream the flowers are fair
That meet one gifted lady's care
With prodigal rewarding ;
But Beauty is too used to run
To Mitford's bower—to want the sun
To light her through the garden.

But, *here*, all summers are comprised—
The nightly frosts shrink exorcised
Before the priestly moonshine :
And every Wind with stoled feet,
In wandering down the alleys sweet,
Steps lightly on the sunshine ;

And (having promised Harpocrate
Among the nodding roses, that
No harm shall touch his daughters)
Gives quite away the rushing sound,
He dares not use upon such ground,
To ever-trickling waters.

Yet, sun and wind! what can ye do,
But make the leaves more brightly show
  In posies newly gathered?—
I look away from all your best;
To one poor flower unlike the rest,—
  A little flower half-withered.

I do not think it ever was
A pretty flower,—to make the grass
  Look greener where it reddened:
And now it seems ashamed to be
Alone in all this company,
  Of aspect shrunk and saddened.

A chamber-window was the spot
It grew in, from a garden-pot,
  Among the city shadows:
If any, tending it, might seem
To smile, 't was only in a dream
  Of nature in the meadows.

How coldly, on its head, did fall
The sunshine, from the city wall,
  In pale refraction driven!
How sadly plashed upon its leaves
The raindrops, losing in the eaves
  The first sweet news of Heaven!

And those who planted, gathered it
In gamesome or in loving fit,
  And sent it as a token

Of what their city pleasures be,—
For one, in Devon by the sea,
  And garden-blooms, to look on.

But SHE, for whom the jest was meant,
With a grave passion innocent
  Receiving what was given,—
Oh ! if her face she *turned then*, . . .
Let none say 't was to gaze again
  Upon the flowers of Devon!

Because, whatever virtue dwells
In genial skies—warm oracles
  For gardens brightly springing,—
The flower which grew beneath your eyes,
  Beloved friends, to mine supplies
  A beauty worthier singing!

THE CRY OF THE HUMAN.

"There is no God," the foolish saith,—
But none, "There is no sorrow;"
And nature oft, the cry of faith,
In bitter need will borrow:
Eyes which the preacher could not school,
By wayside graves are raised;
And lips say, "God be pitiful,"
Who ne'er said, "God be praised."
Be pitiful, O God!

The tempest stretches from the steep
The shadow of its coming;
The beasts grow tame, and near us creep,
As help were in the human:
Yet, while the cloud-wheels roll and grind
We spirits tremble under!—
The hills have echoes; but we find
No answer for the thunder.
Be pitiful, O God!

The battle hurtles on the plains—
Earth feels new scythes upon her:
We reap our brothers for the wains,
And call the harvest . . honor,—

Draw face to face, front line to line,
  One image all inherit,—
Then kill, curse on, by that same sign,
  Clay, clay,—and spirit, spirit.
            Be pitiful, O God!

The plague runs festering through the town,—
  And never a bell is tolling;
And corpses, jostled 'neath the moon,
  Nod to the dead-cart's rolling:
The young child calleth for the cup—
  The strong man brings it weeping;
The mother from her babe looks up,
  And shrieks away its sleeping.
            Be pitiful, O God!

The plague of gold strikes far and near,—
  And deep and strong it enters:
This purple chimar which we wear,
  Makes madder than the centaur's.
Our thoughts grow blank, our words grow strange;
  We cheer the pale gold-diggers—
Each soul is worth so much on 'Change,
  And marked, like sheep, with figures.
            Be pitiful, O God!

The curse of gold upon the land,
  The lack of bread enforces—
The rail-cars snort from strand to strand,
  Like more of Death's White Horses!

The rich preach "rights" and future days,
  And hear no angel scoffing:
The poor die mute—with starving gaze
  On corn-ships in the offing.
                    Be pitiful, O God!

We meet together at the feast—
  To private mirth betake us—
We stare down in the winecup, lest
  Some vacant chair should shake us!
We name delight, and pledge it round—
  "It shall be ours to-morrow!"
God's seraphs! do your voices sound
  As sad in naming sorrow?
                    Be pitiful, O God!

We sit together, with the skies,
  The steadfast skies, above us:
We look into each other's eyes,—
  "And how long will you love us?"
The eyes grow dim with prophecy,
  The voices, low and breathless—
"Till death us part!"—O words, to be
  Our *best* for love the deathless!
                    Be pitiful, dear God!

We tremble by the harmless bed
  Of one loved and departed—
Our tears drop on the lips that said
  Last night, "Be stronger hearted!"

O God,—to clasp those fingers close,
  And yet to feel so lonely!—
To see a light on dearest brows,
  Which is the daylight only!
      Be pitiful, O God!

The happy children come to us,
  And look up in our faces:
They ask us—Was it thus, and thus,
  When we were in their places?
We cannot speak:—we see anew
  The hills we used to live in;
And feel our mother's smile press through
  The kisses she is giving.
      Be pitiful, O God!

We pray together at the kirk,
  For mercy, mercy, solely—
Hands weary with the evil work,
  We lift them to the Holy!
The corpse is calm below our knee—
  Its spirit, bright before Thee—
Between them, worse than either, we—
  Without the rest or glory!
      Be pitiful, O God!

We leave the communing of men,
  The murmur of the passions;
And live alone, to live again
  With endless generations.

Are we so brave?—The sea and sky
  In silence lift their mirrors;
And, glassed therein, our spirits high
  Recoil from their own terrors.
        Be pitiful, O God!

We sit on hills our childhood wist,
  Woods, hamlets, streams, beholding:
The sun strikes, through the farthest mist,
  The city's spire to golden.
The city's golden spire it was,
  When hope and health were strongest,
But now it is the churchyard grass,
  We look upon the longest.
        Be pitiful, O God!

And soon all vision waxeth dull—
  Men whisper, "He is dying:"
We cry no more, "Be pitiful!"—
  We have no strength for crying:
No strength, no need! Then, Soul of mine,
  Look up and triumph rather—
Lo! in the depth of God's Divine,
  The Son adjures the Father—
        BE PITIFUL, O GOD!

LAY OF THE EARLY ROSE.

——"discordance that can accord."
ROMAUNT OF THE ROSE.

A ROSE once grew within
A garden April-green,
In her loneness, in her loneness,
And the fairer for that oneness.

A white rose delicate,
On a tall bough and straight!
Early comer, early comer,
Never waiting for the summer.

Her pretty gestes did win
South winds to let her in,
In her loneness, in her loneness,
All the fairer for that oneness.

"For if I wait," said she,
"Till times for roses be,—
For the musk-rose and the moss-rose,
Royal-red and maiden-blush rose,—

"What glory then for me
In such a company?—
Roses plenty, roses plenty,
And one nightingale for twenty?

"Nay, let me in," said she,
"Before the rest are free,—
In my loneness, in my loneness,
All the fairer for that oneness.

"For I would lonely stand,
Uplifting my white hand,—
On a mission, on a mission,
To declare the coming vision.

"Upon which lifted sign,
What worship will be mine?
What addressing, what caressing!
And what thank, and praise, and blessing!

"A windlike joy will rush
Through every tree and bush,
Bending softly in affection
And spontaneous benediction.

"Insects, that only may
Live in a sunbright ray,
To my whiteness, to my whiteness,
Shall be drawn, as to a brightness,—

"And every moth and bee,
Approach me reverently;
Wheeling o'er me, wheeling o'er me,
Coronals of motioned glory.

"Three larks shall leave a cloud;
To my whiter beauty vowed—
Singing gladly all the moontide,
Never-waiting for the suntide.

"Ten nightingales shall flee
Their woods for love of me,—
Singing sadly all the suntide,
Never waiting for the moontide.

"I ween the very skies
Will look down with surprise,
When low on earth they see me,
With my starry aspect dreamy!

"And earth will call her flowers
To hasten out of doors,—
By their curtsies and sweet-smelling,
To give grace to my foretelling."

So praying, did she win
South winds to let her in,
In her loneness, in her loneness,
And the fairer for that oneness.

But ah!—alas for her!
No thing did minister
To her praises, to her praises,
More than might unto a daisy's.

No tree nor bush was seen
To boast a perfect green;
Scarcely having, scarcely having,
One leaf broad enough for waving.

The little flies did crawl
Along the southern wall,—
Faintly shifting, faintly shifting
Wings scarce strong enough for lifting.

The lark, too high or low,
I ween, did miss her so;
With his nest down in the gorses,
And his song in the star-courses.

The nightingale did please
To loiter beyond seas.
Guess him in the happy islands,
Learning music from the silence.

Only the bee, forsooth,
Came in the place of both;
Doing honor, doing honor,
To the honey-dews upon her.

The skies looked coldly down,
As on a royal crown;
Then with drop for drop, at leisure,
They began to rain for pleasure.

Whereat the earth did seem
To waken from a dream,
Winter-frozen, winter-frozen,
Her unquiet eyes unclosing—

Said to the Rose—"Ha, Snow!
And art thou fallen so?
Thou, who wert enthroned stately
All along my mountains, lately?

"Holla, thou world-wide snow!
And art thou wasted so?
With a little bough to catch thee,
And a little bee to watch thee!"

—Poor Rose to be misknown!
Would, she had ne'er been blown,
In her loneness, in her loneness,—
All the sadder for that oneness!

Some word she tried to say—
Some *no* . . . ah, wellaway!
But the passion did o'ercome her,
And the fair frail leaves dropped from her—

Dropped from her, fair and mute,
Close to a poet's foot,
Who beheld them, smiling slowly,
As at something sad yet holy:

Said, "Verily and thus
It chanceth eke with *us*
Poets singing sweetest snatches,
While that deaf men keep the watches—

"Vaunting to come before
Our own age evermore,
In a loneness, in a loneness,
And the nobler for that oneness!

"Holy in voice and heart,—
To high ends, set apart!
All unmated, all unmated,
Because so consecrated.

"But if alone we be,
Where is our empiry?
And if none can reach our stature,
Who can praise our lofty nature?

"What bell will yield a tone,
Swung in the air alone?
If no brazen clapper bringing,
Who can hear the chimed ringing?

"What angel, but would seem
To sensual eyes, ghost-dim?
And without assimilation,
Vain is inter-penetration.

"And thus, what can we do,
Poor rose and poet too,
Who both antedate our mission
In an unprepared season?

"Drop leaf—be silent song—
Cold things we come among:
We must warm them, we must warm them,
Ere we ever hope to charm them.

"Howbeit" (here his face
Lightened around the place,—
So to mark the outward turning
Of his spirit's inward burning)—

"Something, it is, to hold
In God's worlds manifold,
First revealed to creature-duty,
Some new form of His mild Beauty!

"Whether that form respect
The sense or intellect,
Holy be, in mood or meadow,
The Chief Beauty's sign and shadow!

"Holy, in me and thee,
Rose fallen from the tree,—
Though the world stand dumb around us,
All unable to expound us:

"Though none us deign to bless,
Blessed are we, nathless:
Blessed still, and consecrated,
In that, rose, we were created.

"Oh, shame to poet's lays
Sung for the dole of praise,—
Hoarsely sung upon the highway
With that *obulum da mihi.*

"Shame, shame to poet's soul,
Pining for such a dole,
When Heaven-chosen to inherit
The high throne of a chief spirit!

"Sit still upon your thrones,
O ye poetic ones!
And if, sooth, the world decry you,
Let it pass, unchallenged by you!

"Ye to yourselves suffice,
Without its flatteries.
Self-contentedly approve you
Unto HIM who sits above you,—

"In prayers—that upward mount
Like to a fair-sunned fount
Which, in gushing back upon you,
Hath an upper music won you,—

"In faith—that still perceives
No rose can shed her leaves,
Far less, poet fall from mission—
With an unfulfilled fruition!

"In hope—that apprehends
An end beyond these ends;
And great uses rendered duly
By the meanest song sung truly!

"In thanks—for all the good,
By poets understood—
For the sound of seraphs moving
Down the hidden depths of loving,—

"For sights of things away,
Through fissures of the clay,
Promised things which *shall* be given
And sung over, up in Heaven,—

"For life, so lovely-vain,—
For death which breaks the chain,—
For this sense of present sweetness,—
And this yearning to completeness!"

THE LADY'S "YES."

"Yes!" I answered you last night;
  "No!" this morning, Sir, I say:
Colors, seen by candle-light,
  Will not look the same by day.

When the viols played their best,
  Lamps above, and laughs below—
Love me sounded like a jest,
  Fit for *Yes* or fit for *No*.

Call me false, or call me free—
  Vow, whatever light may shine,
No man on your face shall see
  Any grief for change on mine.

Yet the sin is on us both—
  Time to dance is not to woo—
Wooer light makes fickle troth—
  Scorn of *me* recoils on *you*:

Learn to win a lady's faith
  Nobly, as the thing is high;
Bravely, as for life and death—
  With a loyal gravity.

Lead her from the festive boards,
Point her to the starry skies,
Guard her, by your truthful words,
Pure from courtship's flatteries.

By your truth she shall be true—
Ever true, as wives of yore—
And her *Yes*, once said to you,
Shall be Yes for evermore.

A PORTRAIT.

"One name is Elizabeth."—BEN JONSON.

I WILL paint her as I see her:
  Ten times have the lilies blown,
  Since she looked upon the sun.

And her face is lily-clear—
  Lily-shaped, and drooped in duty
  To the law of its own beauty.

Oval cheeks, encolored faintly,
  Which a trail of golden hair
  Keeps from fading off to air:

And a forehead fair and saintly,
  Which two blue eyes undershine,
  Like meek prayers before a shrine.

Face and figure of a child,—
  Though too calm, you think, and tender,
  For the childhood you would lend her.

Yet child-simple, undefiled,
  Frank, obedient,—waiting still
  On the turnings of your will.

Moving light, as all young things—
  As young birds, or early wheat
  When the wind blows over it.

Only free from flutterings
  Of loud mirth that scorneth measure—
  Taking love for her chief pleasure:

Choosing pleasures (for the rest)
  Which come softly—just as *she*,
  When she nestles at your knee:

Quiet talk she liketh best,
  In a bower of gentle looks,—
  Watering flowers, or reading books.

And her voice, it murmurs lowly,
  As a silver stream may run,
  Which yet feels, you feel, the sun.

And her smile, it seems half holy,
  As if drawn from thoughts more far
  Than our common jestings are.

And if any poet knew her,
  He would sing of her with falls
  Used in lovely madrigals.

And if any painter drew her,
  He would paint her unaware
  With a halo round her hair.

And if reader read the poem,
He would whisper—" You have done a
Consecrated little Una!"

And a dreamer (did you show him
That same picture) would exclaim,
" 'Tis my angel, with a name!"

And a stranger,—when he sees her
In the street even—smileth stilly,
Just as *you* would at a lily.

And all voices that address her,
Soften, sleeken every word,—
As if speaking to a bird.

And all fancies yearn to cover
The hard earth whereon she passes,
With the thymy scented grasses.

And all hearts do pray, ' God love her!'—
Ay, and certes, in good sooth,
We may all be sure He DOTH.

L. E. L.'S LAST QUESTION.

"Do you think of me as I think of you?"
FROM HER POEM WRITTEN DURING THE VOYAGE TO THE CAPE.

'Do you think of me as I think of you,
My friends, my friends?'—She said it from the sea,
The English minstrel in her minstrelsy;
While, under brighter skies than erst she knew,
Her heart grew dark,—and groped there, as the blind,
To reach, across the waves, friends left behind—
'Do you think of me as I think of you?'

It seemed not much to ask—As *I* of *you*?—
We all do ask the same. No eyelids cover
Within the meekest eyes, that question over,—
And little, in the world, the Loving do,
But sit (among the rocks?) and listen for
The echo of their own love evermore—
'Do you think of me as I think of you?'

Love-learned, she had sung of love and love,—
And, like a child, that, sleeping with dropt head
Upon the fairy-book he lately read,
Whatever household noises round him move,
Hears in his dream some elfin turbulence,—
Even so, suggestive to her inward sense,
All sounds of life assumed one tune of love.

And when the glory of her dream withdrew,—
When knightly gestes and courtly pageantries
Were broken in her visionary eyes,
By tears the solemn seas attested true,—
Forgetting that sweet lute beside her hand,
She asked not,—Do you praise me, O my land?—
But,—'Think ye of me, friends, as I of you?'

Hers was the hand that played for many a year,
Love's silver phrase for England,—smooth and well!
Would God, her heart's more inward oracle
In that lone moment, might confirm her dear!
For when her questioned friends in agony
Made passionate response—'We think of *thee*,'—
Her place was in the dust, too deep to hear.

Could she not wait to catch their answering breath?
Was she content—content—with ocean's sound,
Which dashed its mocking infinite around
One thirsty for a little love?—beneath
Those stars, content,—where last her song had gone,—
They, mute and cold in radiant life,—as soon
Their singer was to be, in darksome death?*

Bring your vain answers—cry, 'We think of *thee!*'
How think ye of her? warm in long ago
Delights?—or crowned with budding bays? Not so.
None smile and none are crowned where lieth she,—
With all her visions unfulfilled, save one—
Her childhood's—of the palm-trees in the sun—
And lo! their shadow on her sepulchre!

* Her lyric on the polar star came home with her latest papers.

'Do ye think of me as I think of you?'—
O friends,—O kindred,—O dear brotherhood
Of all the world! what are we, that we should
For covenants of long affection sue?
Why press so near each other, when the touch
Is barred by graves? Not much, and yet too much,
Is this 'Think of me as I think of you.'

But while on mortal lips I shape anew
A sigh to mortal issues,—verily
Above the unshaken stars that see us die,
A vocal pathos rolls! and HE who drew
All life from dust, and for all, tasted death,
By death and life and love, appealing, saith,
Do you think of me as I think of you?

THE MOURNING MOTHER,

(OF THE DEAD BLIND.)

Dost thou weep, mourning mother,
  For thy blind boy in the grave?
That no more with each other
  Sweet counsel ye can have?—
That *he*, left dark by nature,
  Can never more be led
By thee, maternal creature,
  Along smooth paths instead?
That thou canst no more show him
  The sunshine, by the heat;
The river's silver flowing,
  By murmurs at his feet?
The foliage, by its coolness;
  The roses, by their smell;
And all creation's fulness,
  By Love's invisible?
Weepest thou to behold not
  His meek blind eyes again,—
Closed doorways which were folded,
  And prayed against in vain—
And under which, sat smiling
  The child-mouth evermore,

As one who watcheth, whiling
  The time by, at a door?
And weepest thou to feel not
  His clinging hand on thine—
Which now, at dream time, will not
  Its cold touch disentwine?
And weepest thou still ofter,
  Oh, nevermore to mark
His low soft words, made softer
  By speaking in the dark?
Weep on, thou mourning mother!

But since to him when living,
  Thou wert both sun and moon,
Look o'er his grave, surviving,
  From a high sphere alone!
Sustain that exaltation—
  Expand that tender light;
And hold in mother-passion,
  Thy Blessed, in thy sight.
See how he went out straightway
  From the dark world he knew,—
No twilight in the gateway
  To mediate 'twixt the two,—
Into the sudden glory,
  Out of the dark he trod,
Departing from before thee
  At once to Light and God!—
For the first face, beholding
  The Christ's in its divine,—
For the first place, the golden
  And tideless hyaline;

With trees, at lasting summer,
That rock to songful sound,
While angels, the new-comer,
Wrap a still smile around:
Oh, in the blessed psalm now,
His happy voice he tries,—
Spreading a thicker palm-bough,
Than others, o'er his eyes.
Yet still, in all the singing,
Thinks haply of thy song
Which, in his life's first springing,
Sang to him all night long,—
And wishes it beside him,
With kissing lips that cool
And soft did overglide him,—
To make the sweetness full.
Look up, O mourning mother;
Thy blind boy walks in light!
Ye wait for one another,
Before God's infinite!
But *thou* art now the darkest,
Thou mother left below,—
Thou, the sole blind,—thou markest,
Content that it be so;—
Until ye two give meeting
Where Heaven's pearl-gate is,
And *he* shall lead thy feet in
As once thou leddest *his*:
Wait on, thou mourning mother.

ROMANCE OF THE SWAN'S NEST

> So the dreams depart,
> So the fading phantoms flee,
> And the sharp reality
> Now must act its part.
>
> WESTWOOD'S "BEADS FROM A ROSARY."

LITTLE Ellie sits alone
Mid the beeches of a meadow,
By a stream-side, on the grass;
And the trees are showering down
Doubles of their leaves in shadow,
On her shining hair and face.

She has thrown her bonnet by;
And her feet she has been dipping
In the shallow water's flow—
Now she holds them nakedly
In her hands, all sleek and dripping,
While she rocketh to and fro.

Little Ellie sits alone,—
And the smile, she softly useth,
Fills the silence like a speech;

While she thinks what shall be done,—
And the sweetest pleasure, chooseth,
For her future within reach.

Little Ellie in her smile
Chooseth . . . ' I will have a lover,
Riding on a steed of steeds!
He shall love me without guile;
And to *him* I will discover
That swan's nest among the reeds.

' And the steed shall be red-roan
And the lover shall be noble,
With an eye that takes the breath,—
And the lute he plays upon,
Shall strike ladies into trouble,
As his sword strikes men to death.

' And the steed, it shall be shod
All in silver, housed in azure,
And the mane shall swim the wind:
And the hoofs along the sod,
Shall flash onward and keep measure,
Till the shepherds look behind.

' But my lover will not prize
All the glory that he rides in,
When he gazes in my face:
He will say, " O Love, thine eyes
Build the shrine my soul abides in;
And I kneel here for thy grace "

'Then, ay, then—he shall kneel low,—
With the red-roan steed anear him
Which shall seem to understand—
Till I answer, "Rise and go!
For the world must love and fear him
Whom I gift with heart and hand."

'Then he will arise so pale,
I shall feel my own lips tremble
With a *yes* I must not say—
Nathless, maiden-brave, "Farewell,"
I will utter and dissemble—
"Light to-morrow, with to-day."

'Then he will ride through the hills,
To the wide world past the river,
There to put away all wrong:
To make straight distorted wills,—
And to empty the broad quiver
Which the wicked bear along.

'Three times shall a young foot-page
Swim the stream, and climb the mountain,
And kneel down beside my feet—
"Lo! my master sends this gage,
Lady, for thy pity's counting!
What wilt thou exchange for it?"

'And the first time, I will send
A white rosebud for a guerdon,—

And the second time, a glove:
But the third time—I may bend
From my pride, and answer—"Pardon—
If he comes to take my love."

'Then the young foot-page will run—
Then my lover will ride faster,
Till he kneeleth at my knee:
"I am a duke's eldest son!
Thousand serfs do call me master,—
But, O Love, I love but *thee!*"

'He will kiss me on the mouth
Then; and lead me as a lover,
Through the crowds that praise his deeds:
And, when soul-tied by one troth,
Unto *him* I will discover
That swan's nest among the reeds.'

Little Ellie, with her smile
Not yet ended, rose up gayly,—
Tied the bonnet, donned the shoe—
And went homeward, round a mile,
Just to see, as she did daily,
What more eggs were with the *two.*

Pushing through the elm-tree copse
Winding by the stream, light-hearted,
Where the osier pathway leads—
Past the boughs she stoops—and stops!
Lo! the wild swan had deserted—
And a rat had gnawed the reeds.

Ellie went home sad and slow:
If she found the lover ever,
With his red-roan steed of steeds,
Sooth I know not! but I know
She could never show him—never,
That swan's nest among the reeds.

Stories by a Mother:

Containing—Right and Wrong; or, The Story of Rosa and Agnes; and Claudine; or, Humility the Basis of all the Virtues. By the Author of "Always Happy," "True Stories from History," etc. 75 cents; extra gilt, $1 00.

Tales of Domestic Life.

By Mrs. S. C. Hall. Cloth, 75 cents; extra gilt, $1 00.

The Turtle Dove of Carmel,

And other Stories. By Mary Howitt. 37½ cents.

How to Win Love;

Or, Rhoda's Lesson. A Story for the Young. 37½ cents.

The Merchant's Daughter,

And other Tales. By Mrs. S. C. Hall. 37½ cents.

Elements of Morality.

Being Stories for Children. Translated from the German of Salztman. With Illustrations. 50 cents.

Book of Entertainment

Of Curiosities and Wonders in Nature, Art, and Mind, drawn from the most authentic sources, and carefully revised. *Third Series.* Illustrated by more than 80 Engravings. $1 00; extra gilt, $1 25.

The Story of Stories;

Or, Fun for the Little Ones. Being Rambles in the Fairyland of Italy: containing the most popular FAIRY TALES of the 16th and 17th centuries, written in Italy; the original stories and wild conceptions on which the plots of numerous dramas, romantic legends, and best tales of many authors have been formed. With Illustrations by Cruikshank. Cloth, 88 cents.

A Picture Book without Pictures,

And other Stories. From the Danish of Hans Christian Andersen. Translated by Mary Howitt, with a Memoir of the Author. 37½ cents.

Tales of Illustrious Children.

Historical Stories. By Agnes Strickland. With Engravings. 50 cents.

Rose Marian,

And the Flower Fairies. Translated by L. Maria Child With Illustrations. 25 cents.

Bible Cartoons.

Illustrations of Scripture History. From Designs by John Franklin. Containing 16 Engravings of Scenes from the Lives of Adam, Noah, Abraham, Joseph, and Moses, with descriptions in the words of the Bible. 1 vol., 4to. 75 cents.

Ellen the Teacher.

A Tale for Youth. By Mrs. Hofland.

The Scottish Orphans.

A Moral Tale founded on an Historical Fact. By Mrs. Blackford, author of "Arthur Monteith," "Eskdale Herd Boy," etc

The Good Grandmother

And her Offspring. By Mrs. Hofland.

Keeper's Travels

In Search of his Master. Reprinted from the original edition. (In press.)

The Book of Entertainment

Of Curiosities and Wonders in Nature, Art, and Mind. Drawn from the most authentic sources, and carefully revised. *Fourth Series.* With 80 Engravings. $1 00; extra gilt, $1 25.

The Barbadoes' Girl.

A Tale for Young People. By Mrs. Hofland.

Tales from Shakspeare.

For the Use of Young Persons. By Charles and Mary Lamb. With 40 Engravings. $1 00.

Cobwebs to catch Flies;

Or, Dialogues in short sentences. A new edition, re vised and illustrated. 25 cents. Colored, 37½ cents.

The Daisy;

Or, Cautionary Stories in Verse. A new edition, with additional poems. 25 cents. Colored pictures, 37½ cents

The Cowslip;

Or, More Cautionary Stories in Verse. By the author of "The Daisy." 25 cents. Colored, 37½ cents.

Grandmamma's Pockets.

A Tale for Young People. By Mrs. S. C. Hall. 37½ cents.

Hans Andersen's Story Book.

With a Memoir of the Author, by Mary Howitt. 1 thick vol. Illustrated. 75 cents; extra gilt, $1 00.

Wonderful Tales from Denmark.

By Hans Christian Andersen. A new Translation. 1 thick vol. Illustrated. 75 cents; extra gilt, $1 00.

[*These two volumes contain a complete collection of Andersen's Stories for Young People.*]

Gift Book of Stories and Poems.

For Children. By Caroline Gilman. 75 cents; extra gilt, $1 00.

Domestic Tales.

By Mrs. Hofland. Being the Histories of the Officer's, the Merchant's, and the Clergyman's Widows, and their young Families. 75 cents; extra gilt, $1 00.

Mary Howitt's Story Book.

With a Portrait of the Author, and Illustrations. 1 thick vol. 75 cents; extra gilt, $1 00.

Boys' Own Book Extended:

Containing the Boy's Own Book, Paul Preston's Book of Gymnastics, and Parlor Magic; forming a complete Encyclopedia of Sports for Youth. Cloth, $1 25.

www.ingramcontent.com/pod-product-compliance
Lightning Source LLC
LaVergne TN
LVHW010215110826
845151LV00004B/1086
* 9 7 8 1 4 2 5 5 2 7 8 8 4 *